An Economy for All: A More Perfect Union

Gary Taylor

Dedication

For Lacie, Lanie, and Bonnie.
I love you all so much.
And for Edie, Simon, Truman, Lucky,
Matt, James, and Teak.
I love you all.
And for Patience B.
I love you so much,
And I thank you
For helping me learn
To enjoy life again after losing Donna.
And for encouraging me
And working with me
Through this entire project and many more.
And for Donna.
I'll always love you!

Blurb

This book is a collection of short articles, posts, and speeches. The book is multi-purposed, meaning it has multiple intended audiences. My hope is that, taken together, these multiple audiences include everyone. So, the book is for everyone, but for different reasons.

The overall message is one of bringing us together to create an economy that works for everyone, and a nation that works for everyone. While it certainly is an expression of my own opinion, it is fact-based opinion, built on years of study. Among the intended audiences are those who would consider themselves on "the other side" politically. I prefer to think of us as all on the same side. I refer to myself as a Progressive Democrat. My hope is that those who are not Progressive Democrats will learn, from me, what I mean when I use the term. I hope to convince readers that it is a moderate approach and not at all extreme. Incorporating the needs of all are at the core of the philosophy.

Other intended audiences include those who are just fed up with politics in general, and those who consider themselves independents and don't know whom to support. Lastly, I want folks who are already Progressive Democrats to read the book, and particularly Democratic candidates because I believe it has some potentially useful information for you.

So, let me say it again, the book is for everyone: Republicans, Democrats, Libertarians, Independents, Liberals, Conservatives, and the disenchanted. Let's begin to understand each other.

FORWARD

Ending the Divide

In January of 2021, I asked some friends of mine to help me form a group that could meet on Zoom. We were a small group in number, but geographically, we stretched from one coast of the United States to the other, with members in Connecticut, Pennsylvania, Georgia, Minnesota, Texas, and the state of Washington. We eventually called the group "Ending the Divide". My beloved late wife, Donna, and I had tried to start the group in 2016, but were unaware of Zoom at the time, and so we attempted to form a group that would have local chapters that met in person. We called that group "End the Divisiveness". We couldn't seem to get it off the ground due to the logistics of having to find meeting places and recruiting people and getting them to recruit more people, and so, we abandoned the project. In 2020, a little after we lost Donna, I learned about Zoom through some song circle groups to which I belonged that started meeting during the pandemic. With Zoom, it was much easier to organize and the group that Donna and I had hoped to form finally got started.

Through Christy Moore, a member of the group, I learned of the publishing platform, Substack. Betsy Brown, another member of our group, was actually already publishing a great series of articles on Substack at the time she joined the group. She helped me learn more about the platform. Betsy was a great friend of Donna's and mine from our high school days. I had not seen her in years, but somehow learned that she was living in Seattle and was able to reconnect with her. I asked her to join the group and she and her wonderful husband, Jamie Hascall, joined "Ending the Divide" just a couple of months after we started the Zoom group. Sadly, we lost Betsy, too, in 2024.

Once I learned about Substack, I decided I wanted to start writing and publishing a series of "Ending the Divide" articles. With Betsy's long distance help, I began publishing on Substack in 2023. Much of what you read in these pages is pulled from those articles.

This Old Divide

The old divide
Is still alive
It never went away
We need someone to save the day
The list is long of those who've tried
And long of those who've died
Oh why, oh why
This great divide
The nation's torn
Its hope is worn
And patience is running thin
Can all this pain find an end
Why, oh why
This old divide
There should only be one side
And every hate should have to hide
Until it has died
The nation's torn

Its hope is worn
Is the promise gone
No one, alone, can save the day
It'll take us all
And then the pain might go away
Might go away

Available on Spotify and Apple music, Gary Frank Taylor

PURPOSE

A quick outline of my plan and goals for this book:

The primary concept is to present the practicality of building the economy based on the idea of building from the bottom up, but with consideration for everyone. Incorporating the needs of all are at the core of the philosophy.

I will begin by demonstrating what I believe to be a fact—that the current economic structure creates an extremely incorrect, lop-sided distribution of the national wealth (sections 5 thru 8). I will do my best to present convincing evidence of this and simply ask that the reader give it some careful consideration after reading the entire contents.

The main reason for first presenting this defect in the current system, is to then follow-up with the concept that a shift in our national thinking, away from the current trickle-down approach, and toward a model which does indeed have the needs of all at its core, is the correct way to build an economy for all. An economy that retains the positive characteristics of capitalism while eliminating the bad. And there definitely are some bad characteristics and we should not shove them under the rug. There are good characteristics as well, and we should keep them.

This model would begin with the idea of doing everything possible to immediately relieve stress for those who are currently and constantly struggling just to make their way in this world. By all measures this is getting much more difficult with each passing year, particularly for young families. The extreme misdistribution of wealth is at the root of this problem. This extreme misdistribution is the inevitable result of our current economic model—the ultra-pure capitalistic, trickle-down model. Under this model, we are *gifting* entire new fortunes, *daily*, to those who already have unfathomable fortunes. Demonstrating this fact will be a major focus of the book.

We can certainly adjust this system that automatically gives money away to people who don't need it, and are no longer earning it at this point, into a model that works for everyone. Particularly one that works for those who are simply trying to make ends meet and make enough money to pay rent, pay their health insurance premium, buy groceries, buy a car, save for their retirement, save for a downpayment on a house, save for their children's college education, and plan for their own future. They need a much more predictable economic climate in order to plan for the future, and to look forward to it.

This book is an attempt to demonstrate the need for this paradigm shift in public thinking; a shift *away from* building an economy for a few, and *back to* building an economy for all. *And* to show that this is not only the right thing to do, but it is also the practical thing to do. We have somehow lost sight of that practicality, and we must call attention to the fact that there is proof, through precedence, that it works.

I will often call attention to these precedence-setting years when we had a more Progressive tax structure and at the same time, a great economy. These were the years that our country lifted itself out of the Great Depression and built the greatest middle class the world had ever known. That alone is proof that a Progressive tax structure does not ruin the economy.

To be sure, there were still problems, but there was forward movement – progressive movement – even on those issues as well.

Included in this paradigm shift in our national mindset is the recognition that government is not intrinsically bad. Government need not be bad. Bad government is bad. Good government is good. We *are* the government. We can have good government. We must vote for it.

CONTENTS

A Note From the Author

This book is a collection of short articles, posts, and speeches. Several were written as stand-alone pieces and others were written in series. I have taken some time to sequence them, and have edited here and there to make them flow more as a single book. With that in mind, I removed some redundancies that occurred from them being stand-alone pieces, but left others to keep the flow going and to drive home a point. Also, I am using the word "section" for these numbered articles, because they are too short to be called chapters. Occasionally, the word "post" is retained, because many of these were "posts" on social media platforms before they were "sections" in this book. So, posts and sections mean the same thing here.

1. Ending the Divide: Foundational Statement

This first article comes straight from the Ending the Divide Substack page and addresses the philosophy behind the group, including our foundational statement.

We, as a group, believe in the statement given below, and hope that most people do. We believe that most major religions have similar statements as foundational to their moral principles. The statement can be derived from statements very close to universally accepted, self-evident truths. For most people, it ranks as a self-evident truth itself, due to their own upbringing, or perhaps some innate feelings of empathy, or simply a sense of right and wrong. Here is the statement:

All of us should do what we can, both collectively and individually, to make life as good as possible for *all* of us, including ourselves.

For all who believe that we are in the long process of creating a government by the people and for the people—meaning "for all of the people"—then the statement above is certainly self-evident. The statement should, therefore, be a guiding principle when we vote. When we vote, we should consider the needs of all people, not just ourselves, but certainly including ourselves.

We will look upon it as foundational to the continuation of this "American experiment" of creating a nation governed by the people, for *all* of the people.

This statement will guide us in our quest to "End the Divide", and thus continue the dream of forming a more perfect union.

2. Message Specifically for All Voters Under 55

"You are the people who can make a difference in this country."

The future is in your hands right now. I mean immediately. I hope that you will read these pages because I think they can at least offer you some food for thought, and perhaps you can take some of it and run with it. Especially if you can try to make yourselves do it together, in as united a way as possible, while simultaneously celebrating your diversity. Mostly, I think you are the people who can make a difference in this country, and the world. I want all of you to have a great future. I want you to look forward to your future now. As we begin to believe we can have a better future, that belief will be the beginning of a better now.

I believe you can do yourselves, and all of us, a great favor by voting *together*, as a block, for an economy for all. This will be a major step in giving yourselves and your own children a bright, wonderful future to look forward to.

I hope to convince you of this by giving you the reasons for these beliefs rather than just stating the beliefs dogmatically. For a book, I am keeping this quite short. I am making the individual sections short as well, in an effort to make the reading less cumbersome and give the reader time to reflect.

Much of what is presented will be rooted in history, but it is a history that I sincerely believe is relevant to you—to all of us, really. I believe it is knowledge you will find useful and that putting it to use can have an immediate and positive effect on your lives, and your children's lives. (And maybe even your parents and grandparents, while they're still here.)

3. Progressivism

"Progressivism is both compassionate and practical. It is the necessary constant march of humanity."

To readers who, for one reason or another, have a negative feeling about the term Progressivism, I ask that you please read this short book to understand what we who call ourselves Progressives mean by the term. I ask that you learn what we want to do *from us*, rather than from some other source. Once you understand our approach, you can judge for yourself our sincerity and the plausibility of our model. But please take the time to hear us before you make a judgement. There is much misinformation out there these days. I will give the meaning of Progressivism, as I use the word, and my reasons for believing it is the correct philosophy to guide us in forming a more perfect union.

I call myself a Progressive Democrat. I consider it the same as calling myself a New Deal Democrat. I believe in blending the private and public sectors to make an economy for all. Another way of saying it: I believe in blending capitalistic principles with socialistic principles to create an economy that works for everyone. But I will certainly need to explain what I mean by this, because both words, capitalism and socialism, can have positive connotations to some, and negative connotations to others. It is the blending that fixes both.

As a Progressive, I believe in all of us working together as a national community to make life better for all of us. To me, this is essentially what government by the people, for the people means. If the government is "by the people", then that means we are the government, which is equivalent to "all of us working together as a national community". If the government is "for the people", then we are trying to "make life better for all of us".

Progressivism is both compassionate *and* practical. It is the necessary constant march of humanity. A march that must continue as long as oppression exists anywhere, and in any form. I want to repeat, with a slightly different emphasis, that Progressivism is not only compassionate, but it is also *highly* practical, and we, Progressives, need to help people learn this. Progressivism is a commonsense approach to a better economy, a better nation, and a better world.

4. More on Progressivism

"A return to the New Deal model – the Progressive model – can make a better economy for everyone, including those who have, in the past, voted against it."

I believe *all* of us who call ourselves Progressive are compassionate people. I also believe many people who *don't* call themselves Progressives are compassionate people, but they have learned to think that Progressivism is impractical. One of the main reasons for this book is to show this practical side of Progressivism which has not been emphasized in recent years. Many of our ancestors realized it, but they themselves had to try it out in order to convince themselves. It worked, and they were convinced.

I hope to help people convince themselves that the Progressive approach, which is to say, the New Deal approach, works for everybody. I hope to convince people that they are really New Dealers at heart. If they currently believe that it is not practical, I hope to convince them that it is. I think most of us really are on the same side.

I believe that we can work together to create a better economy, a better nation, and a better world. Working *together* is the key. We cannot make an economy that works for *all people*, when we are too dedicated to a model that only works for *some people*; a model that increasingly leaves more and more people out.

We cannot make an economy that works for *all* people if we are too divided in basic philosophy. Recognizing what we must do to make sure everyone is doing okay, economically speaking, and then understanding that we certainly have the means to accomplish it, and even examples to follow, is the first step. It can be a unifying step. Roosevelt thought of it as working from the bottom up. I think that's a good way to think of it. If you make sure that those at the bottom of the economic pyramid, as he aptly phrased it, are getting along fine, then obviously, everyone else is getting along fine (economically speaking, that is).

A return to the New Deal model – the Progressive model – can make a better economy for everyone, including those who have, in the past, voted against it. I believe a deeper dive into its core concepts can help us all understand the benefits to all. I believe we should *all* vote for it in the future. And I believe we can get a large majority to vote for it. This little book is my own attempt to examine those core concepts for myself and for the reader. Again, it's short as far as books go, so I hope you'll stay with me.

5. The Extremely Incorrect, Lop-sided Misdistribution of the National Wealth

"Most of us (well over 70%) would benefit economically from a return to the Roosevelt approach, which I will also call the Progressive approach, or Progressivism. But I also believe that all of us, that is, 100% of us, would benefit from living in a happier, less-divided country."

Higher taxes for those with great wealth has often been described, derogatorily, as a "redistribution of wealth". I believe it is much more accurate to classify appropriate taxation as "correcting a misdistribution of wealth" rather than "redistributing the wealth".

This might be the simplest way to express the need to shift our thinking into using capitalism and appropriate taxation to build an economy for all—one that is fair to all, and good to all. This shift would not be a brand new philosophy. It would basically be a return to the model used from 1933 to 1981, which is essentially the New Deal approach. During those years, we built the largest middle class in history, and we were making continuous gains in building an economy for all.

Under our current economic structure, there are individuals whose wealth increases at a rate of well over 2 million dollars *per hour*, 24 hours a day. This is with no additional effort on their part. This is greater than the combined hourly pay of over 152,000 workers making $15/hour. This is what I mean by a "misdistribution of wealth". This is what needs to be corrected. (The calculations will be presented in the next section.)

Most of us (well over 70%) would benefit economically from a return to the Roosevelt approach, which I will also call the Progressive approach, or Progressivism. But I also believe that *all* of us, that is, 100% of us, would benefit from living in a happier, less-divided country. It will be impossible to ever "unite" on an economy that produces lords and serfs. That will necessarily produce division amongst us. And has. To be more united—less divided, we must unite on the side of an economy for all.

The next few sections will address my belief that we need a paradigm shift in our economic philosophy. Ronald Reagan accomplished a paradigm shift in the 1980s, but I believe, and hope to convince the reader in future sections, that it was a shift in the negative direction; a shift away from a great economy for all. This is not, in any way, intended as an attack on Reagan's character; it is simply a strong disagreement with his economic philosophy. We need to return to the model that builds an economy for all, the Progressive model.

6. Post With Calculations

"A worker making $15 an hour would have to work 76 years to earn what the investor makes in 1 hour. The worker would have to work 1,826 years to earn what the investor's wealth increase would be in a 24-hour day."

I believe that unbridled capitalism (pure capitalism, trickle-down capitalism, laissez-faire capitalism), with low taxes for the wealthiest people, is a system that grossly overcompensates a very few, while underpaying the many and denying basic life necessities and securities for a growing number of people. Let me offer an illustration that goes into more detail on the numbers from my most recent post.

Suppose an individual with a net wealth of $200 billion earns an average return of 10% on their wealth. (This 10% figure is a conservative estimate for this level of investor.)

We multiply $200,000,000,000 by 0.1 to obtain the yearly increase in the investor's wealth. The result is $20,000,000,000. Their wealth increases by $20 billion dollars in 1 year.

Now, let us divide $20,000,000,000 by 365 to get the daily increase in wealth. This comes to $54,794,521 rounded to the nearest dollar. One can immediately see that this multi-billionaire's wealth is increasing at a rate of over 2 million dollars *per hour*. Dividing the result by 24 gives $2,283,105 per hour.

Let us divide this hourly result by $15 per hour to get the number of hours a $15 per hour wage earner would have to *work* to earn, through work, what this multi-billionaire earns in one hour without having to work for it, because their money is earning it for them.

This new result, 152,207, is the number of hours one would have to work to equal the number of dollars the investor's money has earned in 1 hour. This is 152,207 hours of *work*, compared to 1 hour of *nonwork*. Divide this by 40 to get the number of 40-hour weeks a single worker would have to work, and we get 3,804 weeks. Divide this by 50 to get the number of years a worker, working 50 weeks a year, would need to work, and we get 76 years.

So, a worker making $15 an hour would have to work 76 *years* to earn what the investor makes in 1 *hour*. The worker would have to work 1,826 years to earn what the investor's wealth increase would be in a 24-hour day.

I do not use this illustration to turn us against the wealthy, as people; I use it simply to show that the system that produces this situation is not the best when trying to build an economy for all, and a nation for all. Work is extremely undervalued in this system and many, if not most, workers are underpaid.

We must somehow place a reasonable tax on this extreme imbalance caused by pure capitalism. Note that in no way am I abandoning capitalism as a component of the economic structure. I am only saying that it must be tamed in order to provide a good economy for all participants. A reasonable tax on this increase in wealth is not, in any way, a punishment for being wealthy. It is also not "stealing" from the wealthy. It is simply correcting a system that overcompensates already accumulated wealth. An appropriate, progressive tax structure would allow us to put more money back into the hands of those who work for a living. Through the taxing process, the government can quickly put the money back into circulation and it goes round and round again, providing income again and again, for many people.

To me, it is much more correct to say that this ultra-capitalistic approach (trickle-down) "steals" from the workers than it is to say that taxing the extremely easy overaccumulation of wealth for a very few would be "stealing" from these very few.

While there are varying levels of wealth and income throughout the society, even in this trickle-down system, it appears to me that the longer the trickle-down approach is practiced, the more the economy resembles a lords and serfs, medieval-style, economy. Some will be the more favored servants, with higher positions and incomes, and a bit of wealth themselves, but more and more of us will become the modern equivalent of the peasant serfs and become the largest segment of society. And with this situation, "we, the people" will no longer be the government; "they, the lords", will be.

After that last sentence, I feel the need to add again that this is not intended against any individuals, personally, for being the overcompensated. Nor is it to place blame on anyone in particular. Nor is it to presume to know anyone's intentions. It is only an indictment of the system that produces these extreme inequities. And, it is a preliminary to expressing my desire to return to a Progressive, New Deal kind of approach.

7. Regarding the Overcompensation

"If someone is being extremely overcompensated, it follows that others are being undercompensated."

Regarding the wealth increase for the $200 billionaire: If there are any who actually claim that this is not an overcompensation, then I can't help but believe it would have to be for one dishonest reason or another. Or, and this is probably the case for many people, they just haven't thought about it. Neither the enormity of the wealth in the first place, nor the perpetual extreme overcompensation with more and more wealth that follows. It has simply not been called to their attention.

To illustrate the enormity of the $200 billion in wealth for an individual, let us compare $200 billion with $1 million. Imagine a number line with the number 0 on the far left side. If we consider a scale in which 1-inch represents 1 million dollars, then a mark 1 inch to the right of 0 represents a wealth of $1 million. 10 inches to the right of 0 would represent $10 million. If we wanted to place a mark for $12 million, our piece of paper would have to be larger than 8 ½ by 11.

Now, 200 billion is 200,000 times larger than 1 million. So, we would need to make a mark 200,000 inches to the right of 0 to represent a net worth of $200 billion. Divide 200,000 by 12 to get the number of feet to the right. The mark would need to be 16,666.67 feet to the right of 0. Divide this by 5280 feet and we see that on a scale where 1 *inch* represents $1 million, then 3.15 *miles* represents $200 billion. Additionally, the daily increase to this enormous wealth for the $200 billionaire is $54 million, which would be 4.5 *feet* in this scale. Each *day* they are rewarded with 54 times the net wealth of someone with $1 million. With 1 inch representing 1 million dollars, the piece of paper would have to be 4 ½ feet wide to show the *daily* wealth increase for this one individual.

Seriously, it is obviously extreme overcompensation. If someone is being extremely overcompensated, it follows that others are being undercompensated. While it is impossible to know where any line should be drawn, and which particular individuals are being most undercompensated, it is nevertheless easy to understand that those whose income level makes it nearly impossible for them to make ends meet, or to save money, or to keep from going further and further into debt, are among those who should be the immediate beneficiaries of a better constructed system.

If it is to be argued that the super wealthy "deserve" to be tremendously overcompensated because they somehow "contribute" more to society, then the evidence of this "deservedness" would be made plain to us through less economic-caused pain and suffering and hardship throughout the society. If we were to witness a safe and secure population at all levels of the economic pyramid, then we could possibly decide to credit these oligarchs with this concept of "deserving" this enormous compensation brought about by our manmade distribution system. We could say it worked if it created a society with little to no economic hardship. But that is not what is happening, nor has it ever happened. *All* of history shows exactly the opposite. Lord and serf societies always include a large peasant class.

Oligarchic societies are essentially the modern version of lord and serf societies—feudalism. In effect, these super wealthy are a large and unelected part of the government. The longer it continues, the more they become the real government.

The wealth increase in the above example is not *new* investment by the investor which could then possibly be used to create new jobs, or do wonderful things, but also could possibly be used to invent new technology to eliminate jobs, or do not such wonderful things. The wealth increase is simply the return on investments *already* made. It just means the share prices went up, with no new shares being purchased.

Again, this is just to point out a flaw in the system. It is not intended to demonize anyone. I do believe, however, that all of us should recognize what is happening and decide that adjustments must be made, through taxes. Taxes have historically been what poorer people paid to wealthy people. That is essentially what is happening now, in this trickle-down system. The overcompensation is really the same as the working class paying taxes, through lower pay, to the overcompensated. We can turn this around, but in a non-punishing way. The wealthy will still be wealthy, but maybe we can come close to eliminating poverty*, and stress, and economic hardship. We can also improve the standard of living of almost everyone.

Two interesting observations on the misdistribution:

(1) Imagine a long line of people standing in the order of their heights, from left to right, shortest to tallest, and imagine including all people on earth from age 5 up. Then imagine one of the smallest 5 year olds standing next to the tallest person in the world. This is presented just to have you picture the contrast in your mind. The tallest person might be more than 3 or 4 times the height of the 5-year old.

Now, let's imagine a line where we let the heights of people represent net wealth, and let a person 6 feet tall represent a wealth of 1 million dollars. Let's contrast this person with one whose height would represent

200 billion dollars. With this scale, 6 feet = $1 million, we would need to find a person 227 *miles* tall (that's miles, not feet) to represent a wealth of 200 billion dollars, and that person would be growing at a rate of 324 feet per day, compounded at approximately 10% per year.

The point: Nature distributes heights much more equitably than our current manmade economic system distributes wealth.

(2) If we take the combined net worths of the 20 wealthiest Americans and assume a 10.3% return on their total wealth, then their combined net gain in wealth is over 1 billion dollars a day (this is why I chose to use 10.3%; 10.2% doesn't quite make a billion a day). If you multiply by 30, you get a gain of over 30 billion per month. Divide this by $2000, the average amount of a monthly Social Security check, and you see that our system rewards, each month, to 20 individuals, (a number that could fit in a small room) an increase in wealth equal to the monthly Social Security payments of 15 million people. This is not intended to suggest any particular solution to sustaining Social Security. It's just to illustrate a fact and to emphasize an imbalance, and a problem.

These examples, with calculations, are simply to demonstrate that the system, as is, truly does distribute wealth in such a way that it seriously underpays work as compared to what it pays already made wealth. It is a flawed manmade system.

*There are countries that have essentially eliminated poverty by Progressive methods.

8. A More Balanced Approach

"I believe we must have stronger Social Security, and stronger additional social securities, like better and more affordable healthcare, affordable (free?) college education—in effect, an economic system that works for those trying to make their way in this world. This can be accomplished if we return to the New Deal approach—the Progressive approach."

It is this system of ultra-pure capitalism that creates greater and greater wealth for fewer and fewer individuals. Once an individual reaches a certain point, their wealth increase has nothing to do with anything they, themselves, are doing anymore. The system simply gives them more and more wealth (as shown in the illustrations from the previous sections.) They do nothing more to merit this enormous gift that the rest of us bestow upon them. Whenever they do sell some assets and pay a capital gains tax, they are simply paying taxes with a small percentage of the wealth we have gifted them, through this mechanism which automatically pays them more and more. This is, in effect, a tax on all of us. A tax on the system. Additionally, the amount of literal tax they pay never even comes close to the amount of money they are receiving from us.

This is not to take away from anything they may, or may not, have done to position themselves at the mouth of this eternal money spout. They may have done wonderful things of merit to get there. They may have done questionable things to get there. But once there, they don't have to do anything else in order for all of the rest of us to chip in at giving them 54 million or more a day. And again, it's really our money, not theirs. We just created a system that automatically gives it to them. It's on autopilot.

Reiterating, we need a paradigm shift in philosophy—a shift away from this trickle-down system back to Progressivism. We had the paradigm shift in the wrong direction in 1981, after 48 straight years of forward, progressive movement, from 1933 to 1981.

A return to the philosophy that considers working people first, rather than continuing with this philosophy in which our first concern is for the extremely wealthy, seems to me to be an easy choice and one in which a large majority would agree, if they knew what was happening. So, I believe that making sure all are aware of this extreme overcompensation for a very few already extremely wealthy folks is the first step toward more agreement amongst Americans. The second step is to understand what it's doing to us all, both economically and socially.

I think most of us would also agree that, in addition to considering working people in our economic model, it is also correct to include consideration for those who are unable to help themselves. In other words, the emphasis should always be on creating an economy for everybody.

So, I believe it is this ultra-pure capitalistic, trickle-down system, which creates this extreme and ultimately dangerous misdistribution of wealth and resources, that needs to be changed if we want to have a healthy economy for all. We need to correct the misdistribution. We have an earlier American model to follow that worked incredibly well. It retains the good characteristics of capitalism while discarding its negative traits. It builds from the workers, up, rather than from those who have managed to position themselves at the outputs of the money spouts, down.

As stated before, this is not intended to turn us against the wealthy, as people. It is simply to show that the system that produces this situation is not the best when trying to build an economy for all. Work is extremely undervalued in this system and many, if not most, workers are underpaid.

We must also understand that this ultra-pure capitalist system, that grossly overcompensates already accumulated wealth while underpaying work, is no more natural than any other human economic system. The Progressive system is a much more balanced approach in which the needs of all are at the core of the philosophy. It is designed to build an economy for all and leave no one out.

It is worth repeating, the needs of *all* are at the core of the philosophy.

It is important for us to recognize that those with extreme wealth are just as good at eliminating jobs as they are at creating new jobs. Maybe even better. Corporations are great at saving themselves money by employing new technology to replace human workers, thus reducing their payroll while forcing many people to have to search for new careers in the middle of their working years.

I believe we must have stronger Social Security, and stronger additional social securities, like better and more affordable healthcare, affordable (free?) college education—in effect, an economic system that works for those trying to make their way in this world. This can be accomplished if we return to the New Deal approach—the Progressive approach. In the 1980s we turned away from that approach and mostly returned to the model that created the Great Depression. Thankfully, we already had Social Security and Medicare and other Progressive era programs in place to keep it from leading to all out depressions again.

There is a point of diminishing return to the concept that keeping taxes down, particularly on the wealthy, creates a better economy for all. There is no perfect formula for finding that point of diminishing return, but the best gage is to see the effect on those who are simply trying to make ends meet and make enough money to pay rent, pay their health insurance premium, buy groceries, buy a car, save for a downpayment on a house, save for their children's college education, save for their own retirement, etc.

If making ends meet is getting harder and harder for a growing number of people, then the system needs to be adjusted. It's that simple. We have a beautiful precedent to follow.

9. We Can Afford It; It Makes Us Richer

"If you think back to the experiences of the early years of this Administration you will remember the doubts and fears expressed about the rising expenses of Government. But to the surprise of the doubters, as we proceeded to carry on the program which included Public Works and Work Relief, the country grew richer instead of poorer." Franklin Delano Roosevelt

Thus far, I have endeavored to demonstrate the extreme overcompensation of more wealth to a very few individuals who have done nothing to earn this perpetual gift other than having already acquired an extreme fortune. They are rewarded with entire new fortunes daily. This, with absolutely no additional effort on their part, just a modest return on their huge fortunes. This *daily* increase is more than what 99.9% of us accumulate in a *lifetime*. Every day they make enough to place them in the top 0.1%.

Again, this extreme overpayment is a result of our ultra-pure version of capitalism, which is simply a system of human invention. But once invented, we have allowed this unbridled, trickle-down capitalism to run itself with no regard for the people it is supposed to serve. We mostly treat it as though we have no control over it, as though it is nature itself. Or that we shouldn't try to control it, because we think it is natural. But it is a human creation. We need to recognize that it is not serving a large majority very well and would have totally collapsed by now if not for the few remaining safeguards from a previous era.

A secondary purpose of this publication is to demonstrate that it is absolutely false to say we cannot afford the New Deal-style Programs that lifted millions out of poverty (but did not finish the job) and built a huge and thriving middle class for the first time in world history. What we *cannot* afford, if we want to create a good economy for everybody, is a system that continues to make it more and more difficult for working people to make ends meet, while simply dumping whole fortunes, daily, into the laps of those who already have a fortune. In 1938, Franklin Roosevelt said:

"If you think back to the experiences of the early years of this Administration you will remember the doubts and fears expressed about the rising expenses of Government. But to the surprise of the doubters, as we proceeded to carry on the program which included Public Works and Work Relief, the country grew richer instead of poorer."

The New Deal approach actually protects capitalism from itself. These rising expenses of Government actually work to provide a continuous boost to the circulation of currency and provide jobs at the same time. I believe this approach promotes a better environment for free enterprise, while constantly working to reduce poverty, and constantly working to increase the standard of living for most people.

I sincerely believe that the standard of living will increase for a large majority through this means, and I will do my best to give my reasons for this belief in future sections. So far, I have mostly just tried to demonstrate that the ultra-pure capitalist system is way out of balance, and no more natural than a New Deal-style economy. It ultimately hurts many people. It constantly knocks many people down, and then often knocks them down again as they are trying to get up.

I plan, in future sections, to make it clear that the concept of individuals being able to invest for themselves, in a market economy, can and will continue to thrive under a New Deal, Progressive system. It did before.

10. Uniting

"Democrats must unite on getting the message out—on convincing people that we can make things better for all of us."

This section is for everyone, but part of it is specifically meant for Democratic candidates:

Our extreme divide is hurting us all. A corollary purpose of the book is to help unite us as a people; to unite us as a community of diverse people—a national community of diverse people. And to unite us on the things that make a better life for all.

For Democrats, the first work to be done in this area of uniting us all, is to make sure that our own party is united. I say this while believing that we *are* united in heart; we are united in caring; in wanting a better way, a nicer way, a more compassionate way, and a loving way. And we are united in wanting a country where we all take care of each other.

But also, a country that maintains our personal freedoms and our innovative and creative ways, our entrepreneurial ways, our American ways, and within reason – yes, within reason – our system of capitalism. But not an unbridled, trickle-down capitalism that grossly overcompensates a very few while underpaying the many and denying basic life necessities and securities for a growing number of people. Not an unbridled, trickle-down capitalism that runs itself, with no regard for many of the people it is supposed to serve. But a more tamed capitalism: one that includes social securities, like Social Security itself, and affordable, quality healthcare for all. We want an economy that serves us all. An economy based solely on a market structure cannot result in an economy for all. We, Democrats, are already united in all of these things.

Democrats must unite on getting the message out—on convincing people that we can make things better for all of us. Perhaps I should say better for *most* of us rather than for all of us. But in my, perhaps, slightly naïve idealism, I truly think the Progressive approach makes the country better for everybody. I think that that conviction can and should make it easier to convince others.

11. A Self-Evident Truth

"Any concept of building an economy for all must begin with finding ways to immediately assist those who are working hard, but seemingly getting nowhere, or even losing ground."

It should be a self-evident truth that building an economy that prioritizes keeping taxes low for those who benefit most from the system will never result in an economy for all. The concept that this will eventually help all of those who are currently struggling is a huge problem. First, when will this eventuality occur? Will it work in the long run? We've been at it for 44 straight years now. As Harry Hopkins, one of the chief architects of the New Deal famously said, "people don't eat in the long run". There are hard-working people who are struggling now. They need an economy that works for them, now.

If the argument is that this economy, based on keeping taxes down on the top beneficiaries of the system, is not intended to create an economy for all, then that would be truthful. Yes, that would be truthful.

However, if the argument is that it will create the best for the most, we are right back to a false assumption. Both in theory, and in practice, it continuously increases the number of people who are struggling to make ends meet. It decreases the number of people in the middle class. We have basically been following this model since the 1980s. It is hurting many.

Any concept of building an economy for all *must* begin with finding ways to immediately assist those who are working hard, but seemingly getting nowhere, or even losing ground. We begin here, and then determine the tax structure that supports it. Such a structure is bound to exist, as long as there are enough resources to support everybody.

In truth, keeping taxes down, particularly for the extremely wealthy, and then consequently keeping government services down, is a system that will inevitably leave some out. And the logic shows that the longer that program is followed, the greater the number of those who will be left out. History shows it well.

It is government abandoning its job. Let us remember that we, the people, have the power to change it, and we, the people, are the government.

Building from the bottom up was Roosevelt's philosophy. It is a philosophy in which the needs of all are at the core of the philosophy.

12. The Art of the New Deal

As previously stated, my primary purpose is to present a philosophy for building an economy for all, and a nation for all, and demonstrating that that is both compassionate and practical. The playbook already exists for such an economy and nation, and was handed down to us by an earlier generation (1933-1981). We just need to study it, and follow it as a guiding principle. The next generation seemed to take too much of it for granted and many among them lost interest in studying any reasoned attempt to build an economy for all. It seems the majority either believed it would just happen, or believed it couldn't happen. Indeed, most people seemed to have lost interest in even learning that we were actually making great progress toward that end, when we suddenly abandoned the playbook. And they lost interest in studying the methods that were achieving that great progress.

"Just let the economy run itself, that will be what's best for all," became the new mantra. That was easy. You didn't even have to think about it anymore.

But it is a philosophy that implies we have no collective responsibility toward each other. Each man for himself, that's what's best for all. It was the philosophy that gave us the Great Depression; it is a philosophy that ultimately results in a nation of lords and serfs.

13. Uniting on a National Project

"While we may never reach perfection, we can always strive for a more perfect union; one that is constantly dedicated to the ideals of freedom and equality, and may we add to that, the ideals of common goodness and kindness as well."

It was two centuries plus two score and 9 years ago that our fathers brought forth on this continent a new nation, conceived in liberty, and dedicated to the proposition that all men* are created equal.

In 1776, Jefferson had called it a self-evident truth that all men are created equal. But sadly, four score and seven years later, when Lincoln gave his immortal Gettysburg Address, many were saying it was not a self-evident truth. That it was a lie. Thus, Lincoln had to call it a proposition. Both are derived from Euclid. In Euclid's great textbook, known as Euclid's "Elements", a self-evident truth was a statement that did not need to be proved. It was an axiom. A proposition, however, was something that was to be proved, from the axioms. The statement from the Declaration of

Independence was certainly a truth to Lincoln, whether self-evident or not. He often said, "my ancient faith teaches me that all men are created equal".

Of course, both liberty and equality were at stake in Lincoln's time, as was the nation itself; the nation that was so-conceived and so-dedicated, as he called it.

The nation endured, but sadly, the struggle for freedom and equality continue.

What does freedom mean in 21st century America? What does equality mean?

While we may never reach perfection, we can always strive for a more perfect union; one that is constantly dedicated to the ideals of freedom and equality, and may we add to that, the ideals of common goodness and kindness as well.

An economy for all is absolutely required. By this, I mean an economy that is designed to provide security, reduce suffering, and eliminate poverty, to the full extent that these things can be done. I believe it is actually a requirement for democracy itself to truly reach its full potential. It can never be fully realized without it. People without these things are people who are less free.

An economy for all, that provides economic security for all, while simultaneously encouraging innovation and a certain degree of self-determination would indeed be an economy that supports both freedom and equality, as well as democracy.

There is currently a story in circulation which claims that we are not a democracy, that we are a republic. But the truth is, we are both, and always have been**.

An economy based solely on a market structure cannot result in an economy for all. It will necessarily leave many people out. It will necessarily create a segment of society that will live on the edge of financial disaster. Again, this is if the system is based solely on a market structure – an unbridled capitalistic structure, with very low taxes on those who are extremely overpaid by the system, simply because they have already accumulated wealth. It is, essentially, a system with poor circulation. Circulation that doesn't reach the outer extremities of the societal body. It is a system that inescapably causes pain and suffering for a significant number of people, and greatly increases the potential for hardship for even more.

There are many great features of a market-based, capitalistic economic system. But there are also a significant number of negative consequences of such a system. Do we have to accept the bad in order to reap the benefits of the good? Of course not. We can throw out the bad and keep the good. We've done it before, with remarkable success, from 1933 to 1981. And thanks to a few leftover features from those days, we have continued to benefit, albeit not nearly as much, and continuously less, since the 1980s.

I believe that we were once in the process of building an economy for all (1933-1981). That progression came to an abrupt halt in the 1980s. It was then put on a reverse course, where it has since been on track to create great wealth and income inequality, slowly at first, but now accelerating at a mind-boggling rate. But it doesn't just create wealth inequality. It creates poverty and sickness and stress.

A return to the process of building an economy for all would ultimately make life better for all. Much better for all. It would also give us a wonderful opportunity—an opportunity to work on a national project that would serve to bring us together rather than drive us further apart.

**Nowadays we would change that to all "people" are created equal.*

*** Republic vs Democracy: Our country is a representative democracy. That means we are both a democracy and a republic. We elect our representatives. That also means we are both a democracy and a republic.*

There are a few people trying to spread the word that we are not a democracy. We are a democracy and always have been. Our ancestors fought two

World Wars to preserve democracy. The people who fought in those wars would tell you that they were fighting for democracy.

Here is a definition of republic from a 1969 College Dictionary, The American Heritage Dictionary of the English Language:

Republic: 1. Any political order that is not a monarchy. 2. A constitutional form of government, especially a democratic one.

Here is an AI overview from 2025 concerning the nature of our government:

The U.S. is a constitutional federal republic that functions as a representative democracy, meaning citizens elect officials to make laws while being governed by a supreme Constitution that limits power and protects rights. It is not a direct democracy where citizens vote on laws themselves, but an indirect one where elected representatives act on the people's behalf, with checks and balances between legislative, executive, and judicial branches.

14. The Two Philosophies

"The purer capitalistic model overemphasizes the private sector compared to the public sector, in such a way as to limit the ability of government to make the economy better for all. In limiting government, it is actually limiting "we, the people", since we are the government, from crafting a system that benefits us all."

Over the last 104 years, there have essentially only been two basic economic philosophies existing in the United States. In reality, the two basic philosophies go back further than that, but before 1921 they were developing and evolving. By 1921, one of the two philosophies was in place and well-established. The other philosophy did not mature until the full weight of the Great Depression was in the process of crushing the nation.

How to label the two philosophies can be problematic. To me, the easiest way is to call one Roosevelt-style and the other Reagan-style. Of course, the immediate problem with that is that Ronald Reagan was only 10 years old in 1921 when the one I am calling "Reagan-style" was firmly in place. But in 1981 he revived it, so it's somewhat appropriate to call it Reagan-style. I like to think of the two as Progressive (Roosevelt) and Laissez-faire (Reagan). However, I often refer to the Laissez-faire style as unbridled capitalism, or ultra-pure capitalism, or sometimes as a purely market based economy. Both are often described, by their opponents, by more derogatory terms: Roosevelt-style is called tax and spend; Reagan-style is called trickle-down. I have recently taken to calling it lords and serfs. I'm taking the time to write this paragraph simply to clarify that, while all of these labels can become confusing, they really basically just describe only these two philosophies.

The Progressive philosophy can be interpreted as emphasizing more of a blending of the public sector and the private sector into one economy. It can also be interpreted as a blending of capitalism and socialism—or capitalism with social securities. The purer capitalistic model overemphasizes the private sector compared to the public sector, in such a way as to limit the ability of government to make the economy better for all. In limiting government, it is actually limiting "we, the people", since we are the government, from crafting a system that benefits us all.

Summary of the eras:

- 1921-1933: Unbridled capitalism; Reagan-style
- 1933-1981: Progressivism; Roosevelt-style
- 1981- the present: Unbridled capitalism, but with a few leftover Progressive protections

15. The First Turn Around: From Trickle-down to Progressivism

None of us, currently living, have ever had to look for a job during a depression. That is remarkable. I firmly believe this is primarily because of safeguards that were all put in place during the Progressive era, 1933-1981, that began with the New Deal, Social Security chief among them. We owe so much to Roosevelt and his team of New Deal thinkers for creating a positive shift in the thinking of the American voter.

When Franklin Roosevelt became President in1933, the U. S. economy was disintegrating, and the nation was falling apart. From 1921 to 1933, the Republican Party held all 3 branches of government. Within the legislative branch, both the House and the Senate had Republican majorities. The gap between rich and poor grew wider throughout the 12 years, but it accelerated immediately in late 1929 when the stock market crashed. The "official" Great Depression began with the crash, but by the time the crash happened, 60% of the nation was already living on very low wages with many living below the poverty level. The crash accelerated it all by creating a contagion of failed businesses and banks, causing super high unemployment.

The economy was getting worse by the day when Roosevelt took over, but he and his administration, with the help of a Democratic Congress for the first time in 12 years, immediately stopped the slide. Truly immediately. This is not to say that they immediately ended the Depression. But they did immediately stop the downward spiral and literally turned it around. In keeping this short, I will not go into the details of what they accomplished. There is much written about it. I will simply say that by the end of Roosevelt's first term the country was well on its way to ending the Depression and building an economy for all.

Unfortunately, several factors slowed things down during his second term. These factors included the conservative Supreme Court ruling against certain New Deal programs. Additionally, some in Congress, but definitely not all, decided that the worst days of the Depression were over and we could go back to letting the economy run itself without government interference. These factors causing the slowdown in the recovery were all due to *slowing down* on the New Deal concepts. But thankfully, by the end of Roosevelt's second term, the New Deal was back on track. By the time WWII came along, the New Deal philosophy of government participating in employment and the general economy, and in the general welfare of the people, was fully realized.

16. The Second Turn Around: From Progressivism to Trickle-Down

In 1980, Ronald Reagan campaigned on a philosophy of "less government involvement" in the economy. A major component of this philosophy was to lower taxes, particularly on wealthy Americans. All taxpayers saw a reduction in their taxes. But let's put this into perspective. The taxes of taxpayers with lower incomes were reduced enough to afford them a few extra sandwiches per month. Average income earner's might have been able to afford an extra family night out per month. But high income taxpayer's taxes were reduced enough to afford them an additional vacation home, or luxury car, or both. And while the immediate, but temporary, effect would have increased consumer spending, and did do so, the ultimate result would be that that benefit would go to the wealthiest and serve to reduce the relative pay* of the average worker. That has been the actual result with both income inequality and wealth inequality increasing ever since. It is important to understand that this does not just mean poverty-level workers. This reduction over time, in relative pay, is an inevitable result for a significant number of Americans, eventually well over 50%.

*By "relative pay", I mean inflation-adjusted pay, but also pay relative to the costs of living and to the overall wealth of the nation.

17. More on the Paradigm Shift

There exists a popular false dichotomy that only two economic structures exist: pure capitalism or pure socialism. It is often assumed that if you don't support a pure, unbridled style of capitalism, with low taxes on those with the most wealth, then you are a Communist, or Marxist, or Socialist (take your pick, because they are essentially used as synonyms in these accusations).

The truth is there are an infinite number of in-betweens and that both pure systems are fatally flawed. Since 1933, our own economy has been a blending of the two. The relative weights of the two have varied over the years. In more recent years, we have been moving further and further toward a very pure, unbridled version of capitalism, which was the style that ushered in the Great Depression. Thankfully, we still have leftover social securities from an earlier period, namely 1933 to 1981, from which we have continued to benefit, albeit not nearly as much, and continuously less, since the 1980s. I believe that as we allow those safeguards to erode further, that capitalism itself will self-destruct.

Many historians believe that Roosevelt saved capitalism with the New Deal. That is, he saved it through Progressive ideas. I agree with them. I believe, and I believe this strongly, that we should tame our capitalism, which will necessitate some change in our taxation policy, and thereby save capitalism again, as Roosevelt did. I ask my more conservative friends to not then jump to the conclusion that I am a Communist. I am absolutely not! Nor do I know anyone who is. I am running for Congress as a Democrat, and I know many Democrats. None are Communists. Please don't listen to those who say we are Communists, or Marxists. It is not true!

I believe in free enterprise and entrepreneurialism. I also believe we need a strong public sector. I *strongly* believe we need a strong public sector. I will be addressing that more thoroughly in later sections. We must recognize that pure capitalism has both good points and bad. We shouldn't ignore the bad points. That won't make them go away. Pure socialism also has both good points and bad. I believe it is not only correct, but also quite achievable, and desirable, to build an economy that keeps the good characteristics of each, and throws out the bad. And we've done it in the past and were well on the way to perfecting the idea (to the extent that that can happen), when we suddenly reversed course during the 1980s.

As previously stated, I am in no way advocating abandoning capitalism as a component of the economic structure (the word component is important). I mean that sincerely. I am simply advocating a return to the type of economic philosophy we had from 1933 to 1981. Free Enterprise was alive and well. The public sector was alive and well and getting even better for most of those years. We built the greatest middle class the world had ever seen by partnering the private sector with the public sector, and creating things like Social Security, the GI Bill, and great public school systems, which all simultaneously served to encourage entrepreneurialism and free enterprise. I will have more to say about this partnership in subsequent sections, too, but for now, I just say that for all of our lives we have blended the ideas. The blend is being strained now, and moving too far to one side. Both capitalism and socialism are self-destructive in their purest forms.* Our "close to pure" capitalism of the 1920s led to a depression with immense human suffering. Then the blended economic approach pulled us out of it and eventually gave us Social Security and the GI Bill and the means to pay for and win a War against fascism and I could go on and on. These protections have helped prevent all out depressions for 90 years now.

* *When I speak of "pure" socialism, an extreme system, I mean a socialism where there is no entrepreneurialism or free enterprise. Essentially, a system with no private sector. Pure socialism I do not endorse. On the other hand, the philosophy known as Democratic Socialism is more Progressive and New Deal-like, which I do endorse. It includes capitalistic and free enterprise elements.*

When I speak of "pure" capitalism, also an extreme system, I mean a system where, to me, way too much faith is placed in the market to do what's right for people. The market doesn't care whether it is doing right or wrong, it just mindlessly does what it does. A public sector still exists, but for the most part, it is not for the purpose of helping non-wealthy people to survive and build a future for themselves and their children.

Progressivism is neither extreme. It is moderate. It is a blending of the two extremes.

18. The Next Turn Around—Hopefully, the Last: Back to Progressivism

"The previous article gives some degree of foundation, or justification, for my belief that it is absolutely necessary to shift back to a Progressive-style economy, after years of becoming, through the trickle-down approach, more and more feudalistic."

In 1980, when Ronald Reagan pulled off a paradigm shift in the thinking of a large percentage of Americans, it was a shift away from the Progressive approach back to the Laissez-faire approach. He was able to pull it off because too many of the voters were either born after the Depression years, or were too young to remember the suffering of working aged people during the Depression years. They took for granted things like Social Security, the FDIC, and public schools, and they didn't understand the need for a government that cared. In fact, many believed that the government didn't care, or couldn't care. And sadly, for themselves and the rest of us, some even seemed to think that it *shouldn't* care. It is important to realize that those great programs were created by a government that did care – a government by the people and for the people.

Reagan was also able to pull off the regressive shift because people were understandably distrustful of, and frustrated with, government itself after both the Vietnam War and the Watergate scandal. But government is essential. And good government is best.

It is important to understand that there will always be government. Even anarchy will lead right back to government; probably, government by the meanest. It is not government, in and of itself, that is bad. Bad government is bad. Good government is good. The concept of the United States of America is that "we, the people" are the government. We have the power to make it good.

SOCIAL SECURITY

19. Let's Win and Win and Win...

"I want to make the case that we all benefit all of the time from this program, not just when we retire."

Saving the Social Security system and making it even better is of vital importance now, and always. While everyone should vote to strengthen it, it is most important for those under 55 to vote to strengthen it, not just so they can have better benefits when they reach retirement age, but also so that they can benefit now, from its constant stimulus to the entire economy. It is a beautiful system but, I think, often misunderstood.

Since we are a government *by* the people and for the people, it is important for voters to understand how Social Security works—what it is, what it is not—because it is we, the voters, who have the power to continue its success, and make it even stronger.

Social Security was not created to work as a savings account or investment account for individuals. It is an investment for society as a whole. It is all of us investing in each other and for each other. It also promotes free enterprise and entrepreneurialism.

As we each pay into the system during our working years, we are not accumulating money in an individual account. Instead, our taxes are actually providing the present Social Security income for those who have already retired. When those who have already retired were working and paying into the system themselves, their taxes were supporting the retirement of the previous generation of workers. It is primarily a pay as you go system. You do get credit for what you pay into the system, and that figures into your benefit, but you are not building a savings account. It was not designed that way.

A reserve was built up in the early years for both emergency purposes and so that the initial recipients could "earn" the right to future benefits by having first paid into the system. Social Security is essentially an insurance program and the tax paid is essentially an insurance premium. But a great additional benefit is that it is the taxpayers themselves that own the system rather than a few investors who wish to make a profit. Another benefit is that it constantly recirculates currency and stimulates the economy.

I want to make the case that we all benefit all of the time from this program, not just when we retire. I call it a win/win/win/win/win/win/win program (that's 7 wins), but before I explain my reasoning, I want to illustrate one more concept. Social Security is, for the most part, self-sustaining. When the taxpayers pay their Social Security taxes, they are essentially putting money into the pockets of beneficiaries who once paid into the system themselves. When a retiree receives a Social Security check, they usually spend it in the local economy and beyond. They are customers. The businesses that benefit from these customers pay themselves and their employees. These people, in turn, are also customers for local businesses and beyond, and their purchases again support the local and national economies. With each exchange, a portion is paid back to the government in both income taxes and Social Security (FICA) taxes. It can be shown mathematically that essentially all of the money that went out as benefits returns to the government to start the cycle again. The dollars never go away; they just circulate through the system again and again, providing income and purchasing power for many people each time they exchange hands.

20. The Seven Wins

"We all benefit from Social Security from cradle to grave."

The reasons I call Social Security a win/win/win/win/win/win/win program:

- It is a win for the immediate recipient of a Social Security check.
- It is a win for the businesses where those checks get spent.
- It is a win for the employees of those businesses as they both receive a paycheck and have more job security because their employer has more customers.
- It is a win for people who would have had to help support, or fully support, their aging parents had Social Security not existed.
- It is a win for society as a whole because it helps to prevent depressions through all of the above points. FDR knew this when he signed it into law and history has proved him right. Almost assuredly the 2007 crisis would have turned into a Greater Depression than the Great Depression had Social Security and the

FDIC not been created during the Roosevelt years.

- It is a win for society as a whole by allowing people, who otherwise wouldn't have been able to retire, to go ahead and retire, leaving their job for a younger worker, thus reducing unemployment among those who are working-aged. FDR also noted this when the program was instituted.

- Through all of the above items, Social Security works to reduce poverty, all of the time.

We all benefit from this system, all of our lives, not just when we receive the literal, immediate benefits. Social Security guarantees an income for a segment of society. It's like giving them a job. Their job is to spend the paycheck. It guarantees that this segment of society has this job as long as they live, they're never unemployed. This keeps the money circulating and greatly reduces the probability of a contagion of business closures, keeping plenty of jobs for the working aged population.

I truly believe that I have not even listed all of the "wins" here. Many of you may think of more.

Can the system be both sustained and improved? Absolutely! And it would not be that difficult. It would require an adjustment in the tax structure to a more Progressive structure. The easiest first step would be to raise the cap. Beyond that, there are many workable proposals that would both save it for the future, and make it better now, meaning pay better now. We, the people, must understand that taxes fund it, and it is we, the people, who must vote to keep it funded. But those same taxes fund all the benefits listed above, not just the social security paychecks themselves. The taxes we pay are simply all of us making a purchase together. Together, we are purchasing a mechanism for constantly recirculating money and we are purchasing, also together, a stronger, more *secure* economy, thus the name,

Social *Security*. Lastly, we are purchasing a future retirement benefit for each of us individually. We all benefit from Social Security from cradle to grave.

21. More on Sustaining and Improving Social Security

"We must save Social Security, and all of these Wins for the next generations."

As shown before, our current, "low tax on the wealthy" structure, literally "overpays" some people, which is essentially a tax on society as a whole. It's much more of a tax on our overall economy than literal tax itself is to individuals. It requires a significant number of people to be underpaid. This goes far beyond Adam Smith's notion that the capitalist's profit is added to the costs of resources and labor to create the price of a product. This is constant enormous overcompensation without any additional risk on the part of the overcompensated.

While sustaining Social Security, and improving it, will require some people's taxes to go up, I believe it can be done fairly and with no real change in the standard of living for anyone except those whose standard of living *improves* because of an increase in benefits. I also believe that the standard of living of most current taxpayers will improve by the many benefits that we all receive that have been listed above.

The people who currently benefit the most from Social Security are not any of the current recipients. The ones who benefit the most are those whose incomes are much greater than the cap, and accordingly, pay a much smaller percentage of their income than everyone whose income is less than or equal to the cap. Increases in their FICA tax would in no way be a punishment, it would simply be an adjustment to strengthen the system. These taxpayers with incomes far above the cap are currently the greatest beneficiaries, by far, of the benefits listed in the previous section that occur prior to becoming a literal beneficiary. They will continue to benefit even after increasing their taxes, which are unfairly low to begin with. I use the words unfairly low because people with low incomes pay a much higher percentage of their income than those with incomes far above the cap.

We must save Social Security, and all of these Wins for the next generations. They are already paying into it, and it can be both saved and even made better for them. Younger Americans owe it to themselves. Older Americans owe it to their children. We should be leaving a better, more navigable world for each succeeding generation.

22. The Gift of Security

Our ancestors from the 1930s gave us a wonderful gift that we continue to give to each other. A strange, bureaucratic gift that somehow has both heart and soul. A cold, dry, bureaucratic system that somehow finds a way to make a nation of millions able to take care of each other and behave like a family, or small community, or tribe. A family that provides for its children, and with gratitude, simultaneously takes care of those who once took care of us while they simultaneously cared for their aging parents. Social Security is a noble attempt to leave no one out, including those who made mistakes along the way—poor investments, hasty choices, bad career moves, etc.—but all the while, contributed to the community, and were our brothers and sisters.

Social Security is a beautiful blending of the public sector with the private sector. It recirculates, or better yet, continues to circulate the money so that it passes through many hands, counting as income each time. We must vote to sustain it.

23. One More Thing About It

When the program was first started and people were beginning to pay into the system, no payouts were made for the first 3 years so that a reserve could accumulate before any benefits were paid. The reserve continued to build in the early years, since there were so many more paying into the system than there were receiving benefits. Only retirees who had paid into the system were eligible for benefits. This reserve keeps the system safe from collapsing. The reserve is there to give us, the voters, time to determine what to do as life expectancies change and as the ratio of retirees to working aged people fluctuates over time, so that we can keep it strong.

The Social Security System is a great example of all of us doing what we can to help all of us live better lives. It is our constant gift to ourselves—to each other. Let's keep it strong.

P. S. Social Security is not only a retirement plan. It also includes disability, survivor, and family benefits. The above articles focus on the retirement aspect as an example of how it works. The concept extends to these other benefits as well.

24. And, One More (Truly the Last)

"Most importantly, Social Security gives some security to those who, for one reason or another, were not able to accumulate wealth during their working years."

There are many reasons why a strong Social Security program is essential to the economic security and well-being of all people in the nation. One of the most important is that it plays a part in preventing all-out depressions. Social Security was created as a response to the Great Depression, as was the FDIC (Federal Deposit Insurance Corporation). These were designed, in part, to keep people from losing everything during an economic downturn. Soon both programs will be 100 years old. I am convinced that they have prevented us from sliding into a depression several times, but particularly during the 2007-2008 financial crisis, when so many people saw their 401(k)s and retirement portfolios practically disappear. Those people still had Social Security and any money they had in savings accounts that were insured through the FDIC. Had those people lost their Social Security income and their savings, it would have been disastrous for the entire economy.

Another important reason that a strong Social Security program is essential to the economic security and well-being of all is that all Americans are assured of at least some income in their old age. It provides income for people who might otherwise be destitute and dependent on relatives or charities for basic necessities. It helps to prevent homelessness for older folks.

With Social Security, the people who are working (providing labor) are also paying into a system that helps to support the people who are no longer working. This creates a financial structure that matches reality itself. This is what is really happening—some are working, and some are no longer working. The work that we all depend on is being done by the working-aged people. The work of the working-aged people benefits both themselves and the retirees, and so, with Social Security, the finances are set up to do the same.

The retiree is no longer actually working, and therefore is no longer contributing in a literal way. If the retiree built up a small fortune during their working years, then we, as a society and through a human created system, credit them with that, and they are rewarded with a more luxurious retirement than others through their own investments and savings and wealth accumulation. We even give them abstract credit for continuing to support themselves, through their wealth, in spite of the fact that they are no longer actually working. This is not to say that we shouldn't do that, it is simply to point out a fact that this is just due to a system. If it is claimed that their money is still working, we must realize that it is basically working for *them*, not for society at large. There are situations where it could possibly be claimed that their fortune is still working for society at large, but for the most part, they are living off of the returns of already made investments, not brand new earnings being invested.

If the retiree has inherited a small fortune, we credit them in this same abstract way. If they built a fortune through dubious means, we credit them just the same. But their relative luxury of lifestyle, when they are no longer working, is a purely abstract matter based on whichever human-created system has been agreed upon by the society, and based on something in their past, not on any current contribution. As stated in the Win/Win/Win section, anyone who has accumulated wealth has already benefitted from Social Security. They have lived in a society that includes a mechanism for constantly stimulating the demand side of the equation which, in turn, keeps the supply side busy. They have benefited from an economy that has not experienced all out depression.

But most importantly, Social Security gives some security to those who, for one reason or another, were not able to accumulate wealth during their working years. Whatever the reasons, it's too late for them now.

As previously noted, it's an insurance program, but one in which the people, collectively, are the owners, rather than stockholders who are looking to make a profit. Therefore, most of the money that goes in actually goes out as benefits. We all pool our resources to ensure that none of us is flat broke when we retire. While this aspect is "socialistic", most of the people paying into the system are working in the private sector, so capitalism is also still at work, and it is a large part of the equation. Additionally, and perhaps most importantly, the recipients are able to continue being customers for businesses. So, Social Security is a blend of socialism and capitalism, emphasizing the positive aspects of each, while minimizing the negative.

This system will work, and will be there for each succeeding generation, as long as the voters vote to keep it going and to keep it well-funded. When someone claims that it won't be there when they retire, they need to understand that that would only be because the people voted for it to not be there. It would not be because it doesn't work anymore. It is a system that works for all people.

If there were to come a day when Social Security *can* no longer work, it would only be because nothing would work; we will have reached a population distribution for which no system would work for preventing homelessness and extreme poverty. If anything can work, Social Security can. Since it is a system that models reality, it can only fail when reality itself causes the failure—when nothing can physically work.

Lastly, when a person is on Social Security, they have a new job. That is, to spend their Social Security check in the economy. In accountant terminology, it is good for people to consider their Social Security check as a "Last In, First Out" situation. Go spend that check each month in the local economy before you sell any of your assets. Support the economy by keeping the money circulating so others will have an income.

25. An Economy for All

Part 1:

Spending and Income

"A government's finances must be run in almost the exact opposite way of a family's or a business. A government must keep the economy's necessary spending going in order to enable its people to save and have income and prosper. It must also make sure that all get an adequate share."

Almost everyone needs income to survive. Incomes, through a common currency, are the basis of our economy.

Income requires an exchange of money. Spending, in some form or another, must take place. In order for everyone, or at least nearly everyone, to have a decent, livable income, money must continually change hands to create those incomes. In order to have a good economy for all, this continuous spending – which is really serving to continuously boost the circulation of the money that has already been called into existence – must somehow reach everyone's hands often enough to keep everyone out of poverty. Again, this is in order for everyone to receive sufficient income and to have an economy that is good for all. Another dimension that must ultimately be addressed is how to make sure all get a sufficient share of this total societal income.

But while this continual spending among the participants of society is necessary in achieving a good economy for all, because it provides continual income throughout the society, it is also very important to realize that good advice for a young family with an average income might be to save money and be careful how you spend, and not go on a perpetual spending spree. Parents, or heads of households, must think about such things as saving for a downpayment on a house or car, or saving for a college education for the children, or saving for their own retirement, and on and on. Individuals and families must be somewhat frugal in order to someday not have to live paycheck to paycheck. They must try not to let debt overtake them. So, all of this means they must curb their spending to some extent. This is in direct conflict with society's need for the continuous spending throughout the society to provide ample income for all. We need them to spend; we need them not to spend.

Businesses must behave in much the same way as families. They must be careful how they spend money or else they can run into great debt and have to resort to "going out of business" sales.

Governments, however, are quite different in their mission; particularly governments whose aim is to promote the general welfare of all of its citizens, as our constitution specifies. Governments do not need to save for retirement. They hope to exist and work perpetually. They do not need to save for their children's future education; they need to educate their young and old citizens both now and in the future—always. Governments do not need to save for a downpayment on a house; they need to make sure that the citizens themselves can do that, and that the citizens can be adequately housed while they are saving for a downpayment.

Immediately after 9/11, President George W. Bush encouraged families to spend to keep the economy from failing. This was good advice for the sake of businesses, but not necessarily good for the families that needed to save for their own futures. Of course, they should spend in the economy, but they should also save for themselves, simultaneously. The better solution would have included a greater role for the public sector. Perhaps it could have helped to avoid the 2007 meltdown. Instead, many overextended themselves with things like subprime mortgages.

A government's finances must be run in almost the exact opposite way of a family's or a business. A government must keep the economy's necessary spending going in order to enable its people to save and have income and prosper. It must also make sure that all get an adequate share.

And while governments do definitely need to control their debt and not let it grow faster than the inflation rate, they do not need to worry about someday being debt-free. The controlling of debt should always be through appropriate taxation, and never by adding hardship to those who are already suffering.

[*The last time the United States was debt free was 1837, a year in which the economy was actually experiencing the beginnings of a depression. The debt has* increased_*almost every year for the 188 years since 1837. The last time the total debt went down a bit was 1948. A government does not need to try to be debt-free in its old age, because it hopes to never experience an old age. It hopes to never die, and therefore, it hopes to never retire. It is, perhaps, okay for a nation to have a goal of becoming debt-free, but it should never be at the expense of people who are struggling to make ends meet. And it is absolutely unnecessary for it to* ever *be debt-free, as demonstrated by the last 188 years.*]

These two concepts – the necessary spending among the participants in the economy to circulate the currency sufficiently to provide adequate income for all, and the necessary thrift to manage the money for a family, business, or individual – are, as noted, seemingly at odds with one another. Necessary spending; necessary thrift. As the owners of our own government, we, the people, must reconcile these two seemingly conflicting needs. And we can! We have! We even have a brilliantly successful model to emulate: The New Deal model.

Part 2:

A Private Sector and a Public Sector

Albert Einstein: *"Man is, at one and the same time, a solitary being and a social being."*

So, how do we keep the money circulating as rapidly as possible and simultaneously encourage individuals and businesses to save for their future and spend wisely and cut costs? We must not encourage families and businesses to risk great debt, bankruptcy, and ruin, and yet we need the maximum total spending necessary to ensure comfortable, livable incomes for all.

The answer is suggested in these words of Albert Einstein: "Man is, at one and the same time, a solitary being and a social being."

Similarly, the country has at one and the same time, a private sector and a public sector. The private sector corresponds to Einstein's solitary being, while the public sector corresponds to the social being. We must craft our economy to accommodate both. Collectively, we must encourage spending; that is, we must help to make money change hands often so that all can have income. But if too much of that burden is borne by the private sector, it leads to overproduction, excessive consumerism, individuals financially overextended and in debt, and much overall waste due to the need to convince people to buy products they don't need – indeed, oftentimes products they already have, but they just don't have the latest, greatest model – all just to keep the money flowing. It also leads to a very out of balanced distribution, better classified as misdistribution, of the income, and wealth.

It also leads to, indeed guarantees, economic ruin for some portion of society. In addition to the extreme misdistribution of income and wealth, the ultra-pure, unbridled capitalistic system, which includes low taxes on those who benefit most from the system, requires an underpaid class. Furthermore, encouraging the private sector to do almost all of the necessary spending requires people to overspend. It forces upon society a situation where people are constantly tempted to overextend themselves and go into deep debt. It can prevent people from saving and investing for their future and their children's future. It will keep some from ever becoming financially secure.

But thankfully, there is a public sector also. FDR realized this. The public sector can take up the slack because, as noted, the government does not need to save for retirement. There are two great economic roles that we, the public sector, can perform simultaneously to lead to a great economy for all of us, all of the time. These two functions of the public sector can provide the solution to the spend vs. save conflict.

The two functions that we, the people, can perform together, as the public sector, are (1) to employ plenty of people so the private sector does not have to carry as much of that burden and (2) to constantly strive for that employment to be meaningful work that either needs to be done or should be done, but would likely not be profitable for private investment. Included in this goal for meaningful employment can be programs to assist in educating people for employment in fields where there are shortages, or programs to assist in retraining people whose jobs have become obsolete. We need to believe that one function of government is to see to it that all who want to work can have a livable-wage job, and to have a job almost immediately whenever they lose one. When the private sector has difficulty employing everyone at decent, livable wages, doing worthwhile work, the public sector must step in. It will always be doable.

Appropriate taxation is the necessary ingredient. We learned this during the New Deal.

Part 3:

A Constant Boost

"Government spending is actually an act of boosting currency circulation. It adds a whole layer of transactions that keeps the money flowing. It is also simply a case of we, the people, purchasing something together."

Both of these economic roles for the public sector can be accomplished through government spending, which is really simply a gentle, but constant, push to boost circulation of the currency. We should not think of it as money spent, money gone. It's still there, it's just moving from one person to another, and each time it does, it can, indeed should, benefit both the payer and the receiver. It's income for the receiver, and the buyer is getting a good or service in return.

And through sufficient collection of taxes, we, the public sector, get it back again, temporarily, to use it again. Collectively, we, as the public sector, can spend on the things that we, as a society, need. In so doing, we keep the money circulating, thus providing income for many, which, in turn, makes them customers in the economy. That is certainly one of the things that we, as a society, need. As stated, this government spending keeps the spending going so individuals can save. Of course, the individuals will also spend, but their private spending does not have to provide 100%, or most, of the currency circulation.

Government spending is actually an act of boosting currency circulation. It adds a whole layer of transactions that keeps the money flowing. It is also simply a case of we, the people, purchasing something together. A major part of what we are purchasing together is a good economy. But, as also noted, appropriate taxation is the necessary ingredient to make it happen. Government spending keeps the currency moving only as long as enough taxes are collected. It is particularly important to collect enough tax from those who have over benefited, in relation to their contribution, from the system itself. They will still *over* benefit, but not in such an extreme manner. As we have seen, our system of extreme capitalism results in tremendous overcompensation for some. In addition to keeping the circulation going, taxing appropriately is also the way to minimize the borrowing which adds to the national debt.

Part 4:

Constantly Creating Customers

The extremely wealthy often get credit for "creating" jobs, which is certainly sometimes true. But it needs to be understood that they also eliminate jobs. Payroll is usually a corporation's greatest expense, so CEOs are always looking for new technology to replace human beings. And through mergers and buyouts, they often reduce the work force through massive layoffs.

We must remember that "potential customers" is a necessary ingredient for job creation, too. Knowing that a customer base exists can serve to inspire innovation and creativity. Programs like Social Security and various other government hiring and spending programs creates customers for existing and future businesses, keeping private enterprises vibrant and allowing them to keep employing people. It's good for capitalism, and keeps it from being extreme capitalism, which ultimately caves in on itself.

Public school systems are another example of public hiring and spending, creating customers for the local community, and keeping the currency circulating. It would be easy to extend this concept to the college level.

The important thing to understand, and believe, is that a pure market system overpays some and underpays many. Again, that is a pure market system. If enough of us can realize that one thing, agree on it, and wish to fix it, then we can work wonders with the economy and still maintain the positive features of a market system. It should be relatively easy to get most of us to agree on it, because most of us will be better off by it. This was the successful model for the U.S. economy from 1933 to approximately 1968. It continued to be loosely followed until 1981, but from 1968 to 1981 the nation was transitioning back to the trickle-down model that had ushered in the Great Depression. By the 1980s we had essentially returned to that trickle-down theory but, thankfully, held on to some of the programs initiated during the 1930s, '40s, '50s, and '60s. Programs like Social Security, the FDIC, Medicare, Medicaid, the G. I. Bill, and Public Schools.

But all of these programs have gotten somewhat weaker since the 1980s, due to insufficient revenue collection. And all are being threatened now. Threatened by a mistaken axiom – that keeping taxes down on the wealthy creates a better economy for all.

That is wrong in both theory and practice. Always has been. All evidence supports the blended economy approach to achieve an economy for all, and minimize hardship and suffering. The extreme approach, unbridled capitalism with low taxes on the wealthy, creates great inequality and hardship. Hopefully, enough of us can be convinced of that, and that doing away with these vital, New Deal era programs and concepts would be disastrous.

Indeed, keeping these programs and expanding them, and creating new ones in the same spirit, is the way to an economy for all.

Part 5:

A System That Doesn't Care

"A market system does not reward based on any system of morality. It simply rewards – and punishes."

We must examine our economic system closely to begin to arrive at an appropriate tax structure. We must understand that any system is human-made and no more "natural" than any other system. So, we begin by looking at capitalism in its purest form. In its purest form, it is simply an abstract idea. When used as a guide for creating an economy, it creates a system that can, in effect, have a life of its own – a system that has a "nature". We must always remember that this "nature" is still the result of a human-made system, and can be adjusted when it does not result in meeting our needs and goals.

There are many great features of a market-based, capitalistic economic system. There are also a significant number of negative consequences of such a system. Do we have to accept the bad in order to reap the benefits of the good? Of course not. We can throw out the bad and keep the good. We've done it before, with remarkable success from 1933 to 1981. And again, thanks to a few leftover features from those days, we have continued to benefit, albeit not nearly as much, and sadly, progressively less, since the 1980s.

A market system does not reward based on any system of morality. It simply rewards – and punishes. An individual can be well-compensated for a variety of reasons. Some are rewarded for hard work; some, for creativity.

Others are rewarded for greed and stinginess. Some inherit the reward. Many are rewarded for coming up with clever ways to get you to part with your money without really providing much in return. In fact, sometimes they can actually be hurting you individually, or hurting society in general. A few are rewarded simply by already having lots of money, which can produce income for them with little or no effort. They have been able to position themselves at the outputs of the money spouts. Yes, the greatest reward of all comes from managing to position oneself for great reward. Work is the least rewarded in this ultra-pure version of capitalism. There are people who work hard, perhaps even two jobs, but still struggle just to make ends meet. There are also people who are willing to work hard, and often do, but they are not necessarily competitive people. They deserve to make a decent living, free from the stress of always being on the edge of ruin.

Part 6:

Inflating a Bubble

"Keeping taxes down on those with these enormous wealth increases means keeping taxes down on those who are overpaid by the system."

In previous articles I have shown calculations that demonstrate the extreme overpayment of a few that is a result of our ultra-pure version of capitalism. I have shown how the daily wealth increase of some individuals is equivalent to hundreds of years of pay for the average-paid worker.

Keeping taxes down on those with these enormous wealth increases means keeping taxes down on those who are overpaid by the system. This results in many people being underpaid. It is true that capitalism requires some extra benefit to go to true risk-takers, and when this extra benefit is reasonable, it would not need to be classified as overpayment, and therefore would not result in anyone being underpaid. It is the enormous extra payment, with inadequate taxation on it, that results in so many being underpaid.

None of this is to paint the multi-billionaires as evil; it is simply to say that taxing them is not stealing from them, since they are grossly overpaid in the first place. It is correcting a flaw in the system that overcompensates them.

The fact that this is an increase in wealth rather than in reported income is worth consideration and further makes the case. Two main points concerning this fact: (1) we can simply note that the increase in wealth is not only potential income that can be realized when the stock is sold, but it also immediately lays claim to new purchasing power in a purely abstract way, and (2) the fact that it is wealth increase rather than reported income makes the need to do something about it even greater. The 24-hour period of wealth increase previously demonstrated did not mean that over 54 million dollars worth of new assets appeared overnight, it simply means that the price tag on the investments (shares) already owned, increased overnight. It serves to further inflate an abstract bubble that can benefit the wealthiest immediately with buying and borrowing power, and benefit them in the future, when the bubble bursts, because it makes them immune to any crash. But as long as it is just a price tag on some stock, it doesn't get taxed. But it does cause much underpayment for the rest of us. And it keeps us from providing the securities necessary to reduce suffering and poverty, and make the economy work for everyone.

Part 7:

Implement and Adjust

So, what is appropriate taxation? There can be no perfect formula that results in the absolute fairest way to tax. We can always implement and adjust as needed. A tax on these overpaid people should not be considered a punishment, but simply a "correction" to the overpayment. Their overpayment is essentially a tax on the rest of us – a tax on the economy itself. A major goal for us collectively, since "we, the people", wish to "insure [sic] domestic tranquility and promote the general welfare", is to see to it that as few people as possible are suffering. It is our job as social beings, using Einstein's term, and it is our job according to the Constitution.

Throughout history, taxes were something that peasants paid to rich people. This was feudalism. The United States was one of the first nations, if not the first nation, that had the opportunity to turn this around. And at times we have done just that. And have done it extremely well. But the further we venture back into "pure" capitalism, as in the 1920s leading into the Great Depression, the more we are simply reinventing feudalism for a modern society. The overpayment of some, resulting in the underpayment of many, is essentially a tax on the many, even though it is not, literally speaking, called a tax; it is underpayment—underpayment in both income and safeguards. It creates a new peasantry.

Part 8:

Water Trickles Down; Money Trickles Up (Or Maybe It Gushes Up)

"The money was all appropriated for the top in the hopes that it would trickle down to the needy. Mr. Hoover was an engineer. He

knew that water trickles down. Put it uphill and let it go, and it will reach the driest little spot. But he didn't know that money trickled up." **Will Rogers, 1932**

In his "Forgotten Man" Speech of April 7, 1932, Franklin Roosevelt spoke of building "from the bottom up, and not from the top down", and putting faith "once more in the forgotten man at the bottom of the economic pyramid."

Ensuring that those at the bottom of the economic pyramid are safe and secure and making a decent living guarantees an economy for all. If those at the bottom are doing okay, then, by definition, the rest are okay.

In a commencement speech at Oglethorpe University a month after the "Forgotten Man" speech, Roosevelt said,

"But think carefully of the vast sums of capital or credit which in the past decade (the 1920s) have been devoted to unjustified enterprises—to the development of unessentials and to the multiplying of many products far beyond the capacity of the nation to absorb. ...No, our basic trouble was not an insufficiency of capital. It was an insufficient distribution of buying power coupled with an oversufficient speculation in production. While wages rose in many of our industries, they did not as a whole rise proportionately to the reward to capital, and at the same time the purchasing power of other great groups of our population was permitted to shrink. We accumulated such a superabundance of capital that our great bankers were vying with each other, some of them employing questionable methods, in their efforts to lend this capital at home and abroad.

"I believe that we are at the threshold of a fundamental change in our popular economic thought, that in the future we are going to think less about the producer and more about the consumer. Do what we may have to do to inject life into our ailing economic order, we cannot make it endure for long unless we can bring about a wiser, more equitable distribution of the national income.

"It is well within the inventive capacity of man, who has built up this great social and economic machine capable of satisfying the wants of all, to insure [sic]that all who are willing and able to work receive from it at least the necessities of life. In such a system, the reward for a day's work will have to be greater, on the average, than it has been, and the reward to capital, especially capital which is speculative, will have to be less. But I believe that after the experience of the last three years, the average citizen would rather receive a smaller return upon his savings in return for greater security for the principal, than experience for a moment the thrill or the prospect of being a millionaire only to find the next moment that his fortune, actual or expected, has withered in his hand because the economic machine has again broken down."

Roosevelt does not go from one extreme to the other. He still allows for speculative investment. He does not say that we should quit thinking about the producer and only think about the consumer, he says we should think less about the producer and more about the consumer. We are now, essentially, back to those days that preceded the Depression, except for those remaining protections from the New Deal days that have kept us from sinking. I want to call extra attention to one sentence in the above speech of President Roosevelt's:

"Do what we may have to do to inject life into our ailing economic order, we cannot make it endure for long unless we can bring about a wiser, more equitable distribution of the national income."

The above statement is a good summary for much of this book. FDR also mentioned being on the threshold of a fundamental change in our economic thought. The statement above summarizes that fundamental change. I have referred to that as the first paradigm shift. It is long past time to return to that. It should be a permanent shift.

In November of 1932, humorist Will Rogers wrote, concerning the election that Roosevelt had just won over Herbert Hoover and the Republicans:

"This election was lost four and six years ago, not this year. They (Republicans) didn't start thinking of the old common fellow till just as they started out on the election tour. The money was all appropriated for the top in the hopes that it would trickle down to the needy. Mr. Hoover was an engineer. He knew that water trickles down. Put it uphill and let it go, and it will reach the driest little spot. But he didn't know that money trickled up. Give it to the people at the bottom and the people at the top will have it before night, anyhow. But it will at least have passed through the poor fellow's hands. They saved the big banks, but the little ones went up the flue."

Capitalism can serve to inspire innovation and creativity and, in many ways, "make the pie bigger"—potentially for all. But then, it can turn right around and keep many from getting a fair piece of the pie, in spite of their hard work or their willingness to work. But that can be fixed, and the model of keeping the currency circulating, as we did from 1933-1981, is the successful model to emulate.

Part 9:

Recap

Running the finances of a country is not at all like running the finances for a family, or a business. In many ways it's closer to being the opposite than it is to being the same.

A New Deal approach keeps its finger on the pulse of the total economy, and continuously works with the goal in mind of leaving no one out and working for people immediately. With imagination and creativity and dedication to leaving no one out, it can always be done, as long as there are enough natural resources.

Sufficient and appropriate taxation is the key. No one will lose their relative wealth position under an appropriately instituted graduated taxing system. The wealthiest will still be the wealthiest, the mid-wealthy will still be mid-wealthy, the moderately wealthy will still be moderately wealthy, and the least wealthy will still be the least wealthy, but they won't be living in poverty. And they will have more opportunity to pull themselves up. Almost no one will be living in poverty, and everyone will have much more control over their own financial future. Private investment will still exist.

26. We Must Not Be Enemies

As Lincoln said at the end of his first inaugural address *"We are not enemies, but friends. We must not be enemies. Though passion may have strained, it must not break our bonds of affection."*

I published this article in Substack on October 9, 2024. I think it fits in with the other pieces in this book. It was written before most of the other pieces, including the Win/Win/Win article. Many of the articles already presented grew out of this one. I think it is important to include it because there are some slightly different twists in the expression of some topics, but also for the purpose of including the wonderful, beautiful Lincoln quote.

I have many friends and family members who would disagree with me on politics, if they knew my position. I am talking about people that I love and care about. I also have many friends and family members who are on my "side", if that's how we wish to refer to it, in this divide. I would prefer to think that all of us are on the same side, but we all seem to be struggling with that.

I want those friends and family members who disagree with me to know that I believe you are sincere and that you care about the country and what's best for us all. I want those same friends and family members to remember who I am, and believe that I, too, am sincere and care about the country and want what is best for us all.

I have decided to write a series of articles to explain my own beliefs and why I vote the way I do. The purpose is to try to let people know that I arrive at my position after decades of study and careful consideration, and from a sense of caring and compassion for others as well as for myself. But again, I want folks to know that I believe that my friends who vote the other way have also given it much careful consideration and are caring, compassionate people as well. Of course, that's what makes this divide so frustrating for us all. I won't deny that I wish more of you would vote my way. It is a strong desire, because I believe it's what is best for all of us. It is the reason I am writing. I believe we can, and should be, more united. United on a government for all, and an economy for all.

While I certainly realize that no one could ever find the perfect words that would magically bring us all together as one, happy national family of diverse people, I hope I can at least help people understand my own position, and not think of me, and those who agree with me, as the enemy. As Lincoln said at the end of his first inaugural address:

"We are not enemies, but friends. We must not be enemies. Though passion may have strained, it must not break our bonds of affection."

So now, let me say that I am an old-fashioned, New Deal Democrat. I think it's interesting that the words old and New are both in that statement. Old-fashioned sounds conservative, doesn't it? But "New" Deal sounds liberal, or progressive. The U. S., from 1933 to 1981, was a Progressive country, run primarily by the Democratic Party, which held large majorities in both houses of Congress for 44 of those 48 years. The philosophy was that government was *by* the people and *for* the people. This 48-year run began with the election of Franklin Roosevelt. This is the America that existed when I was born, so it is old-fashioned. It was far from perfect, particularly on the issue of race, but it was constantly progressing, even on that issue. And we were certainly the uncontested leaders of the world at that time.

FDR said, "The first obligation of government is the protection of the welfare and well-being, indeed the very existence, of its citizens." That is what I believe.

The great author, John Steinbeck, spoke at a memorial for FDR's closest adviser and the architect of much of the New Deal, Harry Hopkins, shortly after Hopkins died in 1946. At the memorial, Steinbeck reminded us that Hopkins said, "Human welfare is the first and final task of government. There is no other." I love that! It's what I believe.

In 1981, all of that changed. Ronald Reagan had been elected on an ideology that said we should get government out of the way and let the market run the economy with little or no interference from the elected government of the people. What this really means is to let the unelected oligarchs, the multi-billionaires, run the country, at least when it comes to economics. It basically gives us an updated version of the old European-style aristocracies that prompted our American Revolution in the first place.

Throughout history, up until the United States was founded, "taxes" were something that peasants paid to wealthy people (think feudalism). The founding of our country gave the world the first chance to turn that around. By allowing, through capitalism, a chance for people to profit from their hard work and creative ideas, and then give back, through taxes, into that system that rewarded them so well, all can truly benefit.

But, by allowing those whose wealth brings them more and more wealth – whose investments bring them enormous wealth – to allow them to continue to be enormously rewarded without paying a tax relative to their great increase in wealth, we have essentially recreated a system where the poor are paying a tax to the wealthy – it's just not called a tax. Those who are working hard for low pay are being "taxed" by a system of high prices and fewer government services to help them pull themselves up, or to simply live with some amount of economic security. They are greatly contributing to the wealth of the wealthy, but not receiving their fair share in return. The real wealth of the nation is based on its resources and the work of its people. In recent times, as was also true in the Gilded Age, we have allowed some to get a much greater share of this national wealth. And thus, a much greater share of influence in keeping this misdistribution in place.

The Progressive era of 1933-1981 gave us the New Deal, including the CCC and the WPA. It gave us Social Security, the FDIC, the means to pay for and win WW II, the means to pay for and win the peace with the Marshall Plan, a way to prevent sliding back into Depression after the war by creating the GI Bill; they gave us legislation to end Jim Crow laws and make discrimination illegal; gave us voting rights for all citizens, Medicare, Medicaid, higher minimum wages, unemployment relief, an unequaled public school system, and most importantly of all, the great Civil rights acts of 1964 and 1965. It gave workers better conditions and constantly increased minimum wage. All of these were given to us by the Democratic Party. That is their philosophy. The Republican philosophy is to keep taxes down, particularly on the wealthy, and keep government services at a minimum.

If you get a Social Security check, you can thank the Democratic Party. If you wish it was bigger, then vote for those who will fund it properly, which again would be the Democratic Party. Do whatever you can do to help people choose to vote for a large majority in Congress who will fund it properly. The politicians who tell you it won't be there in the future are the same politicians who will not fund it properly. They are the ones who would privatize it, which would essentially take the "security" out of Social Security. The Republican Party always resists funding it properly because they always want to cut taxes, no matter what the tax rate is or what the consequences are. There is much headroom for increasing the benefits now, and simultaneously saving Social Security for future generations, but it does require an appropriate, more progressive tax structure. The amazing thing about it is that it always serves as an economic stimulus. So, it is a beautiful blend of capitalistic and socialistic principles.

So, if you wish your Social Security check was bigger, then please help the Democratic Party regain the majorities that they had from 1933 to 1981, because with the proper, progressive tax structure, Social Security can be made better now, and it can be saved for future generations at the same time. If you don't receive Social Security yet, and fear it won't be there when you retire, then you, too, should help the Democratic Party regain those majorities. They can save it for you. It's also important to understand that this 1935 Social Security Act, and the creation of the FDIC, had much to do with keeping the Great Recession of 2007 from turning into an even Greater Depression than the Great Depression.

Those of us who would like to see a fairer tax structure are not communists; we are not Socialists. But neither do we believe in pure, unbridled capitalism. We believe in a blended economy; one that combines capitalistic ideas with social securities, like Social Security, itself; a system that insures us all, while simultaneously giving each of us as much self-determination as possible. We want to see an economic system that serves us all and helps people when they need it.

I think our system has always been a blend of capitalism with social securities, but in the last 43 years our country has drifted further and further towards purer, unbridled capitalism, which does not create a system that serves all. A large number of people live in constant fear and stress, and many suffer terrible consequences.

If we wish to "End the Divide", (mostly, anyway), it will mean that we need to find ways to unite. I think we can, and should, unite around a philosophy that is designed to eliminate as much stress and suffering as possible for as many people as possible, while simultaneously maintaining as much freedom and opportunity for self-determination as possible. I think this is what the Democratic Party stresses in their platform, and historically they have lived up to it. But in the last 43 years, we, the people, have not given them enough power to accomplish these goals. I do not believe we should unite around an ideology that adds to the stress and suffering of so many.

27. Listening: Uniting the Frustrated

When someone says, "Black lives matter." This is far from even being loud or extremist, in my opinion. But the often-heard response, "all lives matter," is, to me, an expression of "I'm not listening to you, and I don't care about your troubles."

This is also an earlier piece. I published this article in Substack on November 22, 2023. Black Lives Matter had been in the news more at the time.

I am a white, heterosexual male. Since day one of the USA, white, heterosexual males have been more privileged than any other demographic in the country. I personally believe that that is still the case, perhaps not quite as extreme as it once was, but nevertheless, still the case. But I also worry that some are trying to turn the clock back to those times when things were even worse for the less privileged demographic groups. I won't go into all of my reasons for believing white, heterosexual males are still more privileged than others in this section. But I will say here that in our effort to build an economy for all, we must do all in our power to make sure no group has particular advantages over any other. And more importantly, that no demographic is marginalized, and all are safe and secure.

As has been noted by several in our Ending the Divide group, the extremists in our country seem to have the loudest voices. I think that's true. But when I look at these "extremes", I see some as having much more justification in their anger than others. For me, those who belong to a group that has been historically oppressed and marginalized, and that still experiences oppression, injustice, and other types of abuse—those are the ones who have much more justification for speaking out in this way than those who belong to the privileged group(s).

While I believe the expression of their anger can possibly temporarily hurt their own cause, I also believe they have much more right to express their frustration, and we should all listen and try to understand the frustration. A well-known example of this is when someone says, "Black lives matter." This is far from even being loud or extremist, in my opinion. But the often-heard response, "all lives matter," is, to me, an expression of "I'm not listening to you, and I don't care about your troubles." It shows a disregard for someone who has a legitimate frustration, and it does so in a way that shuts down communication and causes even more anger and frustration for the currently, and historically, marginalized Black American. Of course, all lives matter, that is why the reminder that black lives matter is sometimes necessary.

I believe the above is just a small example of the frustrations of many people: Black Americans, LGBTQ Americans, Native Americans, women, and many, many more. White, heterosexual male Americans can have troubles, too, and they (we) need to be heard, but not by attacking any of these marginalized groups. They (we) should join with these groups. I believe in working toward creating a government that is constantly working to improve the lives of all who are suffering.

28. MODERATE VS. EXTREME

"The Republican Party's economic philosophy is that of ultra-pure capitalism. The Democratic Party's philosophy is neither of the extremes. Their approach is a blending of the two. It is moderate."

This, I believe, is absolutely true: There is nothing extreme about Progressivism.

The extreme economic theories are pure capitalism and pure socialism (I am including communism within socialism for this example, even though they are not truly identical).

Progressivism is in the middle. It is a blend. It is moderate. It acknowledges the good and the bad in each and tries to keep the good and throw out the bad.

Progressivism strives for an economic system that serves all people and helps people when they need it. It is about compassion and caring, but also about maintaining our personal freedoms, entrepreneurialism, and free enterprise, within a structure that maintains some balance.

Beyond economic theory, Progressivism is simply about ending oppression.

The words "capitalism" and "socialism" are tough words to use these days, and several have called that to my attention. Neither, in their pure forms, is preferable, nor even sustainable, in my opinion.

I think our system has always been a blend of the two, but in the last 43 years our country has drifted further and further towards purer capitalism, which does not create a system that serves all. A large number of people live in constant fear and stress, and many suffer terrible consequences. In previous sections, I have often referred us back to the years 1933-1981, when the government initiated programs that brought relief from financial stress. Those were years that immediately followed another period of purer and purer capitalism. Those years of purer capitalism, 1921-1933, led to a Great Depression. The following era, 1933-1981, beginning with the Roosevelt Administration, were years when we had a much more blended economy. Great ideas and programs were initiated in those years, and great progress was made. Along with the other great gains, we eventually got Civil Rights Acts passed, which had been a long time coming. That job is not finished. It will never be completed under an oligarchic government. It will never be completed through a trickle-down economy.

I have listed many of the ideas and programs from that 1933-1981, Progressive era here before, so won't do it again now. What I would rather do is call attention to our current situation.

I, personally, do not believe that our two political parties represent two extremes. I believe one is extreme, and the other is moderate. Particularly when it comes to economics. The opposite extreme of ultra-pure capitalism is ultra-pure socialism, or even communism. Neither Party promotes that.

The Two extremes are:

a. Ultra-pure capitalism, with low taxes on the wealthy, which creates oligarchy and a larger peasant class. The larger peasant class is a result of a government that is designed to serve, strengthen, and perpetuate the oligarchy rather than serve and strengthen the people.

b. Ultra-pure socialism which eliminates the private sector all together, and thus eliminates the creativity and innovativeness of free enterprise and entrepreneurialism, and to some extent, the idea of self-determination.

The Republican Party's economic philosophy is that of ultra-pure capitalism. It is one of the extremes.

The Democratic Party's philosophy is neither of the extremes. Their approach is a blending of the two. Particularly those who advocate Progressive policy. It is moderate.

29. Progressivism: The Only Philosophy on Which We Could Ever Truly Unite

I certainly do not believe we could ever *unite* around an ideology that adds to the stress and suffering of many, or any. And yet, that is what we currently have. But then, we are currently *not* united.

We must work to help end this great divide in our country. I believe, strongly, that this will mean to unite us on the side of progressivism, rather than either of the extremes. We must unite on the side that is constantly working to end all oppression.

We can never unite on the side of oppression, because oppression divides. Oppression requires division: the oppressors, the oppressed. Another way to express it is that we cannot unite on the side of oligarchy, because oligarchy requires division. When oppression exists, it is a result of division, and it acts to further divide. The only side on which we can ever truly unite is the side that creates an economy for all, not just for some. That would be a blended economy. That would be Progressivism.

By definition, the purpose of Progressivism is to end oppression, poverty, and marginalization.

I have mentioned that Social Security has worked as a Depression preventer. A more general statement is that *Progressivism* is a Depression preventer. It is also a uniter. It can serve to prevent deterioration in a nation. Ending oppression ends the need for a revolution of the oppressed.

30. Competition

Competition is an important concept within capitalism. But as always, we must be careful with the concept. Competition can be healthy. But competition can also be unhealthy.

Once again, we must recognize that there are negative side effects, and we must not ignore them. Friendly competition can be a good thing. But *friendly* competition would never include impoverishing people. Ruthless competition impoverishes people. Friendly competition can inspire creativity and encourage hard work. Ruthless competition can ruin people economically and cause hopelessness and fear.

A football team could lose every game in a season. But none of the players would go hungry because of it. It is only a game.

Life is not "only a game". Life is an experience that can include games.

A system that includes friendly competition is a good thing. A system that includes ruthless competition is not good. A system that can leave some people hopelessly, permanently, and humiliatingly defeated, and full of fear, is not good.

A system that encourages friendly competition but leaves no one defeated is a good system.

31. Freedom: Another Reason for the New Deal

Abraham Lincoln, April 18, 1864, giving an address in Baltimore:

"The world has never had a good definition of the word liberty, and the American people, just now, are much in want of one. We all declare for liberty; but in using the same word we do not all mean the same thing. With some the word liberty may mean for each man to do as he pleases with himself, and the product of his labor; while with others the same word may mean for some men to do as they please with other men, and the product of other men's labor. Here are two, not only different, but incompatible things, called by the same name, liberty. And it follows that each of the things is, by the respective parties, called by two different and incompatible names – liberty and tyranny.

The shepherd drives the wolf from the sheep's throat, for which the sheep thanks the shepherd as his liberator, while the wolf denounces him for the same act, as the destroyer of liberty, especially as the sheep was a black one. Plainly, the sheep and the wolf are not agreed upon a definition of the word liberty; and precisely the same difference prevails to-day among us human creatures, even in the North, and all professing to love liberty. Hence we behold the process by which thousands are daily passing from under the yoke of bondage hailed by some as the advance of liberty, and bewailed by others as the destruction of all liberty. Recently, as it seems, the people of Maryland have been doing something to define liberty, and thanks to them that, in what they have done, the wolf's dictionary has been repudiated."

In the 21st century, a nation "conceived in liberty, and dedicated to the proposition that all [people] are created equal" is a nation that must be dedicated to ending poverty. People in poverty have less freedom. If we care about freedom, we care about eliminating poverty, to the fullest extent possible. A system that is not *designed* to minimize poverty, but claims it is interested in freedom, is really a system that emphasizes one type of freedom over another type. It emphasizes the freedom for some to harm others over the freedom for all to live in relative economic security. We should strive for freedom *from* oppression, not freedom *to* oppress.

32. It's a Wonderful Life

In the Frank Capra holiday classic, *It's A Wonderful Life*, there is a scene where Ernie, the cab driver, says to George and Mary, *"Don't look now, but there's something funny going on over there at the bank, George. I've never really seen one, but that's got all the earmarks of a run."*

During the 4 years immediately prior to Franklin Roosevelt's presidency, over 9000 banks failed. There were "runs" on the banks where depositors would all race each other to the bank to get their money out while they still could. Of course, the banks don't keep all that money on hand. They lend it out. That's their primary business. So, the first people to show up got their money, but eventually, as more people showed up, the bank would run out of money and have to close the doors. Many people lost their life savings, and the people of the United States lost all faith in the banking system.

Franklin Roosevelt's first inauguration was March 4, 1933. Two days later, on March 6, he announced a bank holiday that was originally scheduled for 4 days, but then extended to March 13. On March 12, he gave the first of his famous fireside chats and explained the banking situation to the public over the radio. He assured people that the banks that would reopen first were safe, sound banks. This helped restore people's faith in the banking system and many people re-deposited their money in the banks. They preferred using a bank rather than keeping their money under the mattress.

On June 16, 1933, just a little over 3 months after Roosevelt took office, Congress passed the Banking Act of 1933, and Roosevelt signed it into law. This act established the Federal Deposit Insurance Corporation (FDIC). Along with Social Security, this has been a major factor in preventing depressions. The deposits of the individual depositors are insured, up to a given amount. In addition to insuring people's deposits in the case that their bank fails, it also makes the failures themselves less likely in the first place by helping to prevent runs on banks. People didn't rush to the bank to get their money since they knew it was insured. FDR and Congress were dealing with emergency situations, and performed incredibly well. In addition to making immediate improvements in the economy, they established long-term safety nets, like the FDIC and Social Security. We have had recessions, but we have not had a major depression since the Great Depression. We owe much to the New Dealers.

Back to *It's a Wonderful Life*: Shortly after noticing the run on the bank, George Bailey went to his own office at the Bailey Building and Loan and worked a little magic to keep the doors open. He said, "Don't you see what's happening? Potter isn't selling, he's buying."

This line demonstrates, through the art of movie making, a fact about the extremely overcompensated beneficiaries of our trickle-down system. They are crash proof. George Bailey goes on to say that Potter is picking up bargains. When people panicked, Potter, the richest man in town, started offering to buy people out at low prices. This is the case for our current over-compensated folks. If we were to experience a major crash, many of us would lose our nest-eggs, while the overcompensated could afford to buy a bunch of low-priced stock. If you're withdrawing $4000 a month from your 401(k) and the market crashes, you either have to live off of a lower monthly withdrawal, or watch your balance get closer and closer to 0. When the market comes back up, you may not have much left in there to grow it back.

Ever since the Reagan years, a significant percentage of voters have "bought in" to the idea that the economy works best if we don't make wealthy people pay much in taxes. That has been the defining feature of the Republican Party's economic philosophy. Coupled with that defining feature is the idea that government services for the non-wealthy should be minimal.

We are quite fortunate that Social Security and the FDIC still exist, and we have the New Dealers to thank. We should follow their lead on healthcare (and many other issues).

33. On Healthcare

Of the wealthiest, free nations of the world, the U. S. has the lowest life expectancy and the highest per capita expense for healthcare (by a long-shot). We're spending much more money to live shorter lives. The nations that do better include all of the Western European nations, as well as Canada, Australia, the United Kingdom, and many more. For us, insurance companies receive a huge number of our healthcare dollars. That is the difference. A significant number of our healthcare dollars goes to insurance company CEOs and stockholders, while we simultaneously have a shortage of medical personnel.

I believe that the expense of our system and the shorter life expectancy in our nation are both rooted in this profit driven insurance system and our trickle-down economy. But once again, I want to say that the overhauling of the system, which I strongly believe is needed, should be done with care for the workers who currently work in the for-profit health insurance industry, to help them transition, if necessary, into new jobs. We need affordable, quality, healthcare. No one should have to go bankrupt due to getting sick, and no one should have to choose to go uninsured just so they can pay their rent. But we need to make the transition as smooth as possible and not cause chaos within the whole economy. But at the same time, make changes to help people immediately. I have faith that it can be done, and we will all be better off for it. Once again, a deeply divided country cannot make this happen. We must unite and vote for it, as we, the people.

People who "buy in" to the Reagan economic theory are "buying in" to the idea that keeping taxes down on wealthy people helps them provide more jobs. Of course, this theory did not originate with Reagan; it was also the theory of the 1920s, and has been at the heart of conservative economic philosophy all the way back to the Gilded Age.

And while there is, perhaps, a grain of truth in the theory that wealthy people provide jobs, we know they also eliminate jobs. These days, with bots and robots and AI and the internet, corporations can, and often do, cut their workforce and payroll to increase profit for their stockholders. That practice of cutting the workforce to increase profit existed well before the current hi-tech age, but it is even more prevalent now. Additionally, throughout time, without the push of government and/or unions to raise minimum wages, shorten the workweek, and give employees other benefits, corporations usually do what they can to keep wages low, number of hours worked high, and the capital spent on employee benefits low. They often try to cut their expenses by hiring contract labor, and thus not providing benefits at all for workers. Not all employers do this, but many do. We, as the government, could actually make it easier on employers and employees with better healthcare and retirement benefits offered by "we, the people".

We should go back to the Roosevelt philosophy, but be sure to include everybody this time.

FDR said, in his April 14, 1938, Fireside Chat:

"If you think back to the experiences of the early years of this Administration you will remember the doubts and fears expressed about the rising expenses of Government. But to the surprise of the doubters, as we proceeded

to carry on the program which included Public Works and Work Relief, the country grew richer instead of poorer."

In theory, stimulating the economy through government spending works, and if we look to the example of the New Deal years, the WWII years, the GI Bill years, and the Cold War era, we see that there is plenty of evidence to support the theory. It works in theory and in practice.

But there is one more factor needed to balance the equation: the taxes collected must be sufficient to keep these programs afloat. In the years cited, the tax rate was sufficient. That changed during the Reagan Administration when the highest income tax bracket was cut drastically, from 70% to 28%*. This was an immediate, enormous boost for the people with the highest incomes. But it hurt the rest. Not immediately. But it was the beginning of the movement toward greater income inequality, greater wealth inequality, and harder times for the average family to simply make ends meet. Wages did not keep up with the cost of living. That is getting worse at an ever quickening pace.

*Prior to the 1980s, income tax was a much more progressive, graduated structure. The Reagan era tax cuts represented a major change in philosophy and re-introduced the trickle-down system of the 1920s. That, coupled with relatively low capital gains taxes have led to both income inequality and wealth inequality. As we have seen, wealth inequality has really gained speed now, as exponential functions do. It must be addressed in a tax system that can return us to our New Deal quality of life improvements. Again, not as punishment, but simply correcting the extreme misdistribution of wealth.

34. More United—Less Divided: Right and Wrong

This is another Ending the Divide article, first published on Substack November 3, 2023

In keeping with our foundational statement:

"All of us should do what we can, both collectively and individually, to make life as good as possible for all of us, including ourselves."

We believe the United States should be more united—less divided. On issues where people suffer at the basic levels of human needs there should be no division, at least in the desire to make things better for the people who are suffering and wronged by the system in place. We should expect large majority agreement on these basic issues.

Lincoln once said, "If slavery isn't wrong, nothing is wrong." Slavery was/is an issue for which there should be no middle ground. It's wrong. We think, or at least we hope, most people nowadays would agree. That is, a large majority would agree. But in Lincoln's day, that certainly wasn't the case (among white people, that is). And there were people, like Stephen Douglas, who actually tried to take a middle ground approach. But Lincoln recognized that that was, in fact, a pro-slavery approach. Again, slavery is either right or wrong; there is no middle. And, of course, it is wrong!

We think we have issues like that now, issues for which there should be no middle ground. They might not be so clear to us as the slavery issue. However, a deeper look into them could bring them into focus and make them clearer for us. There are issues where the wrong approach can hurt people and have a negative effect on their quality of life, at a basic level. Those are issues for which we should make a united effort to solve, and as quickly as possible. Those are issues on which we should be more united.

We are currently divided over Progressivism vs Trickle-down. And for years now, that divide has been relatively close to 50-50, swinging back and forth a bit over the last 44 years. This 50-50 situation, with the swinging back and forth, ultimately favors the oligarchy. It favors wealth over people. It favors wealth over work. Extreme wealth wins in a 50-50 election. It defeats democracy. It probably wins even in a 60-40 divide, when it's the 40. The divide makes no sense for a people who choose their own representatives. A large percentage of people who are siding with oligarchy, are voting against their own best interest. We all get a better nation if we are more united. If we wish to be more united (70% or more), then by definition, it must be on the side that is not based on division.

We *can* be united on Progressivism, because it creates an economy for all, not just for some. It is built on the concept of ending oppression and including everyone – leaving no one out. It is built on a unifying concept.

35. Vote for Us: Vote for a Platform that Works for Us

"I have said that I believe at least 70% (probably closer to 80%) of Americans would be better off, economically, if the current Democratic Platform could ever be realized. But most Americans don't know this."

What should we do? We, as in we, the Democrats. But also, we, as in we, the people of the United States. We, as in all who care about making life better for all, not just for some. We who believe we are all in this together. We who want to eliminate as much pain, suffering, and stress as possible for all people. And we who believe that we should do this for each other, as well as for ourselves. We, as in those of us who accept the "Ending the Divide" foundational statement:

"All of us should do what we can, both collectively and individually, to make life as good as possible for all of us, including ourselves."

I believe we should quit the negative campaigning or, at least, greatly reduce it, on both "sides", (I prefer to think of us as all on the same side, but it is what it is, or should I say, we are where we are). We need to spend much more time telling people why they should vote for us and much less time attacking individuals on "the other side". I think it is fine to point out why we disagree with a philosophy, particularly economic philosophy, and why we think our approach is better. I wouldn't put that in the category of negative campaigning.

We, who are Democrats, should also be very honest with ourselves and realize that we cannot truly deliver on any of our promises without both the Presidency and super large majorities in the House and the Senate. Until we win large majorities in both the House and Senate, and keep them, and at the same time win the White House, the best we can hope for is to slow down the extreme right movement toward oligarchy. I believe, with full conviction, that this hurts Republican voters, too. Things are getting continuously worse for *most* people who work for a living.

How do we win super large majorities? By first, *believing* that we can. By believing that we can convince people that their lives will be better if they, the people, vote for the Democratic Party. I say the Democratic Party because they are, in general, the Progressive Party. To any extent that they are not, that needs to change. They/we need to fully embrace Progressivism and the New Deal theories. I think they/we, the Democrats, mostly have.

This means we need to begin a campaign to convince everyone that we possibly can convince– including, and maybe even particularly, those who currently vote Republican – that we can make their lives better and their country better. Of course, we can't convince all of them, but we can play percentages and try to convince as many as possible by creating a message that informs them; a message that explains to them *why* we think their lives will improve, *how* we think their lives will be improved, and how their stress levels will be lowered if Democrats can truly be given the chance to deliver on the issues. Democrats need a message that lets Republican voters know that we *respect* them and believe we are working for them, too.

Democrats haven't really had the power to deliver since the 1970s, as is shown in the chart in the appendix. I have pointed out many times that Democrats had the majority in both houses for almost 48 straight years from 1933 to 1981. But an additional point must be made: The last time the Democrats had the majority in *both* houses for more than 2 consecutive years was in the late 1970s. They really can't be blamed for much because they haven't had power long enough to accomplish much or deliver on the issues. The only things they can be blamed for is not convincing enough people to vote for them – not convincing enough people that their platform has the practical solutions to our national problems. Presidents Clinton, Obama, and Biden, only had majorities in both houses for the first two years of their presidencies. This is why we have had trickle-down since the 1980s. Republicans have had their say over economic policy for most of the last 44 years.

I have said that I believe at least 70% (probably closer to 80%) of Americans would be better off, economically, if the current Democratic Platform could ever be realized. But most Americans don't know this. I think we should work together to educate ourselves and each other. We need to learn how to articulate why we believe in the Democratic platform and why we believe that most people, if they knew it and understood it, would also want to vote for the Democratic platform. I believe that the current Republican Party, based on their economic philosophy, should never get more than 30% of the vote. If this would ever actually occur, as I sincerely believe it should, then they would begin to change their own economic philosophy, and become more Progressive. If there are going to be exactly 2 major parties, then both should be Progressive when it comes to economics.

For any voter who feels stuck in a low wage job and can't see a way out, and believes he or she is being underpaid, a vote for the Republican Party would be a vote to continue the system that necessarily underpays a portion of the population. Not voting at all, would essentially be the same. But also, even voters whose incomes are in the 70th percentile are typically just one disaster away from extreme economic conditions.

The chart in the appendix gives information that all Democratic candidates need to know. It is also information that all voters need to know – voters on both "sides" and voters on neither "side". A quick summary is this – America once had a 48-year run of Progressive government, one in which the wealthy paid a much larger share in taxes while the government instituted programs that greatly reduced poverty.

By the end of that run, they had even finally made great gains against Jim Crow laws which previously had made it possible for businesses to discriminate and bar black people from restaurants, hotels, buying houses in certain neighborhoods, and more. Unfortunately, that battle is still not fully won, particularly when it comes to housing and justice.

As shown in the appendix chart, this Progressive era was 1933-1981. Democrats held majorities in both houses for all but 4 of those 48 years. Republicans held the White House during part of this period (16 of the 48 years), but the era belonged to the Progressives, via the Democratic Party. Republican presidents were more progressive back then, too. But the Democrats owned the day. And once again, look at the accomplishments of that period.

The government of 1933-1981 improved people's lives. It was a government that helped people help themselves while simultaneously stimulating the economy. It was a government that paid for these things with an appropriate tax structure. It was a governmental and economic model that worked. The only thing that ever slowed it down at times was those who resisted the model.

36. Messaging: Something to Work On

We need a vote for us movement, instead of a multitude of vote for me campaigns.

We must work together to make government work *for* us again. We seem to have lost sight that we have this ability.

I believe it would be wise for the strategists, leaders, campaign managers, etc., of the Democratic Party to reevaluate their strategies. They need to realize that since 1981, while winning perhaps 50% or more of all elections and patting themselves on the back for each victory, they have not been winning (much) on the issues themselves. We have been living in an increasingly trickle-down economy since the 1980s.

I believe that we, as a party must regain our past, glorious legacy. We are the party that gave the nation Social Security, the FDIC, the Works Progress Administration, the Civilian Conservation Corps; we brought electricity to rural America; we gave the nation the methods and means to finance and win WWII, a war against fascism, and the way to win the peace after the war.

We gave the nation the GI Bill to help build a new, huge and thriving, middle class, the greatest the world had ever known, and to keep us from sinking back into the Depression after the war; we gave the country the political and economic climate to build great public school systems and universities and a Supreme Court that gave us the Brown vs the Board of Education ruling, abolishing the separate but equal ruling which was certainly separate, but never equal; we gave the nation the minimum wage and any of its raises over the years; we gave the nation Medicare and Medicaid, and finally, and most importantly of all, the great Civil Rights acts of the 1960s.

All of these were initiated and brought about by the Progressive, Democratic Party!

How did they do it?

They held majorities in the House and the Senate for 44 of 48 years from 1933-1981. Let me repeat that because I think it is so significant. The Democrats were the majority party for almost 48 straight years! All of these things were accomplished during that time. Since then, Democrats have not been able to accomplish the big items like that long string of accomplishments from 1933-1981. Why?

Because since then, Democrats have not held majorities in both houses for more than two consecutive years. That's right. After almost 48 straight years as the majority party in both houses, Democrats have not had any significant power in Congress for more than two consecutive years since the 1970s. And if you don't have significant power for more than two consecutive years, you don't really have significant power.

I don't like using the word power here. Progressive policy is not about power; it's about making a country and an economy for everyone. Republican philosophy is about power; it is about giving power to a few. Democrats have had 3 presidents since the 1980s, but those presidents had to work with an oppositional Congress for most of their presidency. No great Democratic strategies have had the opportunity to take hold since 1981.

It is my very strong opinion that this information is just as important for people who have voted Republican any time since the 1980s as it is for the leaders and candidates of the Democratic Party. Any dissatisfaction with the economy over the last 44 years is a dissatisfaction with Republican, trickle-down economics. Since the election of Ronald Reagan in 1980 and the added boost to trickle-down from the Newt Gingrich-led 1994 Contract with America, we have only had remnants of Democratic economic philosophy from the previous 48 years. Republicans have had the majority say-so for the last 44 years.

None of the great accomplishments listed above were products of the Republican Party. All of the Progressive era accomplishments resulted in a growing middle class with greater security, and a healthy environment for people who worked for a living.

The Republican economic philosophy is generally against these programs. As we know, it is essentially one of keeping taxes down on the wealthy and of *not* creating programs to directly help working people, or people living on the edge of unexpected financial disaster. Their philosophy does not include direct help for the non-wealthy. The only direct assistance the Republican philosophy ever gives to working people is to lower their taxes by a few bucks while simultaneously cutting services for them and giving huge, significant tax breaks to ultra-wealthy folks.

The real tax cuts go to those with high incomes and wealth. The small tax cut for the non-wealthy actually does nothing to help them catch up as they get further behind due to a rising cost of living. The accompanying large tax cut for the wealthy serves to increase the rate at which the non-wealthy are getting further behind. This is not to say that some don't find their way out. But that number is shrinking.

Republican economic philosophy will only ever give direct assistance to employers, not to lower wage income earners, or workers. The employers might create new jobs, they might not. There are plenty of layoff-happy employers in existence.

Businesses understandably keep costs down when they can. This is not a judgement for or against. It's just stating a fact. Payroll is typically their greatest expense. Keeping wages down, keeping number of employees down, and reducing the need to provide employee benefits by using contract labor when possible, are all ways that businesses keep costs down, in an effort to maximize their profit, or sometimes just to stay in business. None of this is to the benefit of the average worker.

All of these things hurt people. While it makes sense for the employer, it hurts many employees. It is not necessarily immoral of the employers to do these things, and it is even understandable when realizing they are trying to maximize profit, or to simply stay in business. But I do question the morality of then choosing to deny the government the funds to provide benefits and securities for these workers, and for all people.

An overall Progressive tax structure would not hurt the businesses that are struggling, but it would help the *people* who are struggling, particularly if we put those dollars to use specifically for that purpose. That is the act of building from the bottom up, of which FDR spoke. It is designed to leave *no* one out. The Progressive taxation, of which a graduated income tax would be a major component, solves the problem.

[Note: Some advocate a flat tax. While I would consider it as a possibility, it would not be my first choice or recommendation. I believe it would probably have to be fairly high in order to deliver an economy for all, including the safety nets and securities for all workers as well as help for people down on their luck. I think there are countries that have had success with it, but it is a very high flat rate. It also would not address our already extreme wealth inequality situation. I believe a Progressive, graduated system is probably preferable, particularly when considering wealth as well as income.]

We, all of the people, need Progressive Democrats to win large majorities in both houses, like they did in the glory years of the party. Democratic strategists need to quit running individual campaigns and run campaigns for majorities. It is the *only* way to win on the issues and win for everyone. They need to realize that they must have majorities in both houses again, and then keep them forever. They need to campaign hard everywhere, and believe that all districts are winnable.

I repeat. They need to believe *all* districts are winnable. Remember, the last time Democrats had the majority in both houses for more than two consecutive years was in the 1970s.

Below is an excerpt from a speech I once gave to a small Democratic club:

"So, when I say we need to unite the party, I don't mean on the issues, because I believe we are mostly united on those already. What I do mean is we need to speak with one voice, and it must be a unifying voice, and a welcoming voice; one that even welcomes those who have voted against us in the past. One that aims to unite people rather than divide.

We need to organize and work together as a unit, all over the country. We need to run a single "vote for us" election, instead of a multitude of "vote for me" elections. We need to be contagious, electrifying, and even entertaining!

But always show our love and compassion mixed with our practicality and common sense.

So, in an effort to not only build a better future, but also create a better now, I am committed to working with *all* Americans toward ending the great divide in the country."

Government can make a beautiful, wonderful, positive difference in people's lives, and has many times. We must work together to make government work *for* us again. We seem to have lost sight that we have this ability.

The word government itself is misleading for a country where "we, the people" are the government. The word "govern" sounds like you are being controlled. But self-government means self-control. Theoretically, at least, any person who wants to run for office, can. Anyone who wants to be a part of the government can be. And anyone who wants to participate can participate by voting. Abraham Lincoln was amazed that he, a very poor, frontier-born, self-educated "nobody", could be chosen to be the leader of this great country. We pick our representatives, and each of us has the ability to try to be one. But we all have a say. And in a Progressive, "Economy for All" structure, we can all have pretty close to an equal say. Not true in "an economy for some" structure, which is to say, an oligarchic economic structure. That is not a one person, one vote reality.

37. An Unnecessary Battle

"As Einstein says, we are both solitary beings and social beings. We need our individual freedoms, and we need to work together for each other. We need free enterprise and social security—social security in a broader sense than just the current program. Social security in the sense of greater economic security for all."

In their purest forms, capitalism and socialism appear as opposites. I believe it is a mistake to think of them that way. It causes an antagonism where none need exist. I prefer to believe that they are not mutually exclusive. In fact, each is the complement to the other, and no system can be successful at making life as good as possible for all of us unless it contains elements of each.

Capitalism encourages freedom of enterprise, creativity and inventiveness, and when held in check, a spirit of friendly competition and perhaps, fun. Socialistic principles make sure no one is left out and no one is truly suffering in a country with plenty of room for all and resources for all. The socialistic principles, in turn, work to keep the economy from stagnating and only working well for an increasingly small number of people. They actually create a better economic environment for enterprise.

This blend is, in some sense, what we already have. For instance, we have stock markets, restaurants, coffee shops, automobile makers, airplane manufacturers, computer chip makers, software companies, and the list goes on and on. These are all examples from the private sector and of capitalistic principles. We also have Social Security, public schools and universities, interstate highways, public roads, Medicare, Medicaid, Federal Deposit Insurance, unemployment benefits, police departments, fire departments, and on and on. These are all examples from the public sector and of socialistic principles.

The question becomes one of exactly how to blend the two ideas and make them actually one concept with several parts and a common goal. A concept that works toward achieving the goal of making life as good as possible for all of us.

In 1949, in an article called, "Why Socialism?", Albert Einstein wrote, "Man is, at one and the same time, a solitary being and a social being." Later in the same article, he wrote: "Man can find meaning in life, short and perilous as it is, only through devoting himself to society."

Einstein's words support the goal of our Ending the Divide foundational statement. Indeed, they were an influence in creating the statement: "*All of us should do what we can, both collectively and individually, to make life as good as possible for all of us, including ourselves.*"

As Einstein says, we are both solitary beings and social beings. We need our individual freedoms, and we need to work together for each other. We need free enterprise *and* social security—social security in a broader sense than just the current program. Social security in the sense of greater economic security for all. Throughout history, we have allowed wealth to accumulate in the hands of a few, and the rest have had varying degrees of economic well-being, ranging from comfortable and secure, to abject poverty—hopeless poverty. Throughout this same history, charity and philanthropy have existed, but never have they even come close to eliminating the extreme suffering and extreme poverty.

Government programs have done much better, both here and in other countries. I applaud charities and philanthropists. I also applaud a government that can take the concept further, and do more, and work toward the goal of creating an economy and country for all.

In making life as good as possible for all, eliminating extreme poverty *must* be a goal. After all, why not? There can be no good reason for why that should not be a goal. While it may be impossible to fully achieve, we should always be working toward that goal, aiming to get as close as possible. Good government is a necessary element.

As a self-governing people, the surest way we can deliver on the economic well-being of us all is through our self-governing process itself.

38. A Great Reason (to End the Divide)

I believe we need to End the Divide for the sake of ourselves, our children, our grandchildren, and yes, for some of us, even our great grandchildren. Of course, we can never expect full agreement on everything, or maybe I should say, on anything. But I think we need to *believe* the extreme divide can be overcome, and we should all work hard to make it happen. To me, this does not mean that we "compromise" on everything. There are issues for which compromise *is* the answer. But I believe there are extremely important, major issues on which we can, and should, find large majority *agreement*, with no need for compromise; issues for which we should be united, not divided. Large majority agreement meaning 70% or greater.

How do we identify these issues? Simply this: They are the issues for which there is both continued suffering and new suffering if solutions are not found.

Let me say that again: the issues on which we should find large majority agreement are those for which there is both continued suffering and new suffering if solutions are not found.

Progressivism is simply the idea of all of us working together to solve those problems. In both theory and practice, it has the added benefits of building a robust economy for everyone, including entrepreneurs, and of making everyone more secure.

And in the act of bringing us together, it works to end the extreme divide.

39. Concerning Our Foundational Statement

"We need to believe we can end the extreme divide."

A further explanation of the statement below:

"All of us should do what we can, both collectively and individually, to make life as good as possible for all of us, including ourselves."

When we say all of us should do "what we can", we mean to imply that all of us should do what we can, "within reason". The phrase, "including ourselves", should help to convey this. We want to enjoy our own lives and simultaneously do what we can to ensure that others are enjoying their lives as much as possible, too.

Economic security and healthcare are two areas where we have the ability to make a huge difference for each other. The more we work collectively on this, the greater the chances of success, and the easier it should be for all of us. The more divided we are, the more difficult it will be.

Two "sides", with nearly equal numbers, fighting over how, or even whether, it should be done, certainly makes it more difficult. The divide is working for those who don't believe we should help each other in this way—those who believe it should be "every man for himself" and that there will be inevitable losers and that it is their own fault that they are the losers.

When the Great Depression hit bottom, Roosevelt and company realized that it wasn't the fault of those who were "losing". We didn't reach super high unemployment levels because a bunch of people suddenly got lazy and didn't want to work. It was due to a contagion of business and bank failures. As more people lost their jobs, more businesses lost customers. It was the system that was failing. Not the working people.

The divide gives the top 1% (in wealth and income) the power to basically force the bottom 70% to live on the edge of security and disaster *all of the time*. The 29% not accounted for in these stats probably come out fine either way, so it would be nice (kind) for them to join with the 70%.

We need to believe we can end the extreme divide. And again, while we know we can't expect full agreement on everything, we can certainly achieve large majority agreement on those issues that matter most. A quick explanation for why the large majority agreement should be 70% or greater is based on our foundational statement given above.

The spirit and intention of the statement means we should certainly help those in poverty, both immediately and in ways that will help them no longer be in poverty. But the statement includes "ourselves". If we, ourselves, are not in poverty, then of course, part of our motivation is to help those in poverty. But not by hurting ourselves or anyone else. One more time – we need a better blended economy – one that blends capitalism and socialism in such a way that maximizes the good effects of each and minimizes the bad.

Some statistical research convinces me that at least 70% of the people are one disaster away from extreme economic hardship. A quick look at the 70th percentile for income should be convincing. Even people whose income is greater than that of 70% of the population are at an income level that is difficult for building security and getting beyond a paycheck to paycheck existence.

To change this, we need this better blended economy. All of us should vote for this better blended economy, but for at least 70%, it could help alleviate much stress. That 70% should certainly be united, not divided, at election time.

40. Welcome to Ending the Divide

The divide, as I see it, has existed since the beginning of the country. I am not naïve enough to believe we can hope to ever completely end it, but I am naïve enough to believe that we could end much of it and make life better for each other.

While the divide has always been with us, there are times when it is much worse than at other times. And for the sake of our children, we need to figure out a way to minimize its effects for generations to come.

In a letter to Albert Hodges, a Kentucky newspaper editor, Lincoln wrote, "I am naturally anti-slavery. If slavery is not wrong, nothing is wrong".

At first glance this may seem like a simple statement of the obvious. Obvious nowadays, at least. But the more I think of it, the more profound I think it is. Lincoln was a thorough, logical thinker. Here he says, "If slavery is not wrong, nothing is wrong." Implied in that statement, is that there is a such thing as right and wrong. And here he gives the specific case that can convince us all. We all consider slavery wrong if we are the one to be enslaved. We don't need our religion, or any particular religion, or any particular authority to tell us this. Slavery is an obvious issue for which compromise is NOT the answer. You can't be in the middle.

What would it mean to be neither pro-slavery nor anti-slavery? Would a compromise between pro-slavery and anti-slavery parties end slavery and end the suffering caused by it? Being in the middle on this issue would mean you don't think it's wrong. The issues that are like that for us now, might not be quite so obvious to us, but they still exist and are apparent when given serious thought. These are any issues for which compromise would necessarily mean continued suffering for some of the population.

Once we fully understand these issues, we *should* be able to *agree* on what's right and what's wrong, at least on these major issues. Those issues should have no middle ground. So, I would like to reiterate—issues where human suffering and fear and immense stress are at stake—these are the issues over which we should NOT be divided. These are the issues for which there *should* be large *majority* agreement.

41. A Little More on Messaging

We need messaging that serves to unite people rather than divide them. Divisive messaging works for those who need enemies. It seems to work for those who wish for power and/or extreme wealth, and to preserve the status quo for those who already have power and wealth.

We should work on expressing and presenting ideas and philosophies, founded on logic, that benefit the whole of society instead of some parts of society over others. Then we need to figure out ways to spread the message. We want to let people know what we think and why we think it, without being confrontational. We may occasionally be controversial, but we want to refrain, to the best of our abilities, from being confrontational.

Opposition politics can produce short-term results, like winning an election. But opposition politics does not produce long-term objectives, like achieving a safe and secure economy for all.

We don't want to make enemies. And we do want to help those who, for some reason, believe we *are* their enemies, learn that we *are not* their enemies.

We must end the extreme division. We, the people, should be more perfect in our union.

42. Eye on the Prize: Ending the Divide Through the Issues

"I believe that if "the people" understood that, and understood the Democratic platform better, they wouldn't be so divided. Of course, getting the people to listen is the hard part. But also wording the message correctly needs to be examined."

This is from a Substack post from June 2024:

By now, most of you know that, for me, Ending the Divide means we must become more united on the issues. And most of you know that I support Democratic candidates. So, I am writing this from a Democratic point of view, but in a spirit of friendship for those with a different point of view.

It is important for all of us, but particularly for Democratic candidates, to recognize that winning elections is the "means to an end", but not "the end" in itself. Winning on the issues is "the end". Winning on the issues is the real goal.

I think we need to keep this in mind – always. And with this end in mind, we must try very hard to understand what it will take to make it happen. It requires much more than just winning individual elections. It requires getting large majorities and keeping them for a long time. We must convince people to join us because it is what they want, too. We will win huge majorities once this convincing has occurred. The strategy itself must be to win majorities, not to just win winnable districts. That hasn't worked in over 40 years.

During the glory years, 1933-1981, Democrats held the majority in both the House and the Senate for 44 of the 48 years. They got a lot done!

But in the past 44 years, Democrats have won many elections, pretty close to 50-50 with the Republicans, but not enough to deliver on promises. On the major issues we make little, if any, real advancement. We occasionally move a little bit forward, mostly don't move at all, and sometimes we actually move backwards. We can't move forward if we, the people of the United States, are so divided. A divided people elects a divided government.

I believe that if "the people" understood that, and understood the Democratic platform better, they wouldn't be so divided. Of course, getting the people to listen is the hard part. But also wording the message correctly needs to be examined. We need to get out the vote, as we always work to do, but we also need to *turn* votes in order to gain large majorities and keep them, and to build a more united people. We must believe that we can convince people that we can build a fairer, stronger economy, as the platform says, and make their own lives better and less stressful. And we must believe that together (united), we can make these things happen. Divided, we cannot.

To achieve an economy for all, we need a more united Congress, which will require a more united electorate. This will, in turn, require a vigorous, persistent effort to unite people around the issues and the candidates. It will require working to educate ourselves and others, on the issues. And yes, it will require us to turn votes. Obviously, we cannot change everybody, but I think we can change enough, and I believe that we can, and should, get large majorities – and keep them for a long time. But to do this, I believe the strategy must change, at least somewhat. And we must begin by convincing those who have supported Republicans that we are not their enemies. And we are not Communists. We win on the issues by winning large majorities. We must work together.

43. More United—Less Divided Part 2

"There was even a picture in my senior yearbook of a sign that said, 'Save your Confederate money boys, the South's gonna rise again.' In the core of my being, I knew this was all wrong. We were commemorating and glorifying something that was very wrong."

The Civil Rights struggles of the 1960s, as well as my own personal experiences growing up in Texas, then moving to New Jersey during some very formative years of my life (ages 13 through 16), and then back to Texas, all served to influence my full choice, by 1980, to be a liberal, or a Democrat, or a Progressive, or whichever word we wish to use. I turned 16 in 1970, and spent the '70s figuring out what I believed, but always tended toward the liberal side. That word is not used so much anymore, but I think it still describes my views. As you can see by this book, I am choosing to use the word Progressive, but I think of liberal and Progressive as much the same. Words used as political labels gain multiple and incorrect, and often derogatory, meanings over the years, so we have to try to let people know what we mean when we use them.

At an early age I somehow had developed some concern for the situation of black people in America, both then and throughout history. The Texas school district in which I grew up was still segregated when I moved to New Jersey in 1967 at age 13. One black student had tried to come to our elementary school for a few weeks, but quickly changed his mind. I hated to see some of my friends make fun of him, but I don't think I said anything to them at the time. I had other friends who treated him well.

The school in New Jersey was integrated. I had my first experiences going to school with black students and playing on an integrated football team. Martin Luther King, Jr. was assassinated during my 3½ years in New Jersey. All of America was trying to understand this issue that had been an embarrassment and contradiction to our "land of the free" from the first day the United States had existed as a nation.

When we moved back to Texas in November of 1970, we moved back to the same town and school district that we left 3 and a half years earlier. The district had finally integrated and had closed the once all-black school. I attended the newer high school that was on the south side of town. The school had a southern theme, with a Confederate-themed mascot, Confederate school flag, Confederate-themed drill teams, and a school newspaper called the Plantation Times. The fight song was to the tune of Dixie. There was even a picture in my senior yearbook of a sign that said, "Save your Confederate money boys, the South's gonna rise again."

In the core of my being, I knew this was all wrong. We were commemorating and glorifying something that was very wrong. But I played my heart out on that Confederate-themed football team and got into the school spirit with everyone else. There were about 4 black students on the football team. I got to be pretty good friends with one of them because he and I were the only guys that were on both the football team and in the choir. I always wondered how he felt about playing on a team with a Confederate-theme, but I never got up the nerve to ask him. Sadly, he died at age 42, so I can't ask him now.

I bring all of these things up simply to say that I believe the issue of Civil Rights, more than any other single thing, is what made me a Progressive. It is also the issue that made me an avid student of history, although that was not my major in college. But I have made up for it since then.

I think the divide has existed since *day one* of this country. It was over the issue of slavery. And when chattel slavery was finally abolished, the divide reinvented itself with Jim Crow laws and lynching and racism.

When Ronald Reagan accomplished the paradigm shift in the thinking of many American voters that resulted in lowered taxes for wealthy Americans, and a new allegiance for unbridled, trickle-down capitalism for many Americans, I believe it set the forward progress in civil rights on a course of slowing down, and then turning around. I am not accusing Reagan of doing that on purpose. I don't know what his intentions were. But I would like to make this observation:

An economic system that rewards extreme wealth with more wealth, and rewards already accumulated wealth thousands of times more than hard work, is a system that keeps money and power where it is when it takes hold. No one can argue that America was a white supremacist nation during the slavery days, and continued to be so on through the Jim Crow days. The hard work of the many brave Civil Rights leaders going way back in history and continuing through the 1960s had finally brought black Americans the *beginning* of the opportunity to fully participate in the American economy, and to live the American Dream. And to see, in the future, the possibility of the beginning of the end of white supremacy.

I believe that unbridled capitalism makes that dream impossible.

Wealth mostly stays where it is and grows at an ever faster rate, where it is. I do not accuse anyone in particular of intending the results of trickle-down capitalism for that purpose, but I do believe that it should, at the very least, be realized that it is the result, whether intended or not.

(I feel compelled to say that I do believe that *some* of its proponents are bound to have intended it, but I don't want to make any particular accusations. I prefer to give individuals the benefit of the doubt, and hope they will come to realize that continued white supremacy is a result of trickle-down economics and that it is a form of systemic racism, and choose to join us in ending it.)

Race should not divide us. Issues over race should not divide us. A thorough study into the effects of the past on the conditions of today reveals that there are effects of slavery that linger to this day and effects of Jim Crow laws that persist to this day. For centuries, a whole segment of the American population was denied property, the opportunity for education, often times denied staying together as a family, and denied any accumulation of wealth to pass on to their children and grandchildren.

The difficulties encountered by people due to the influence that both the slavery past and the Jim Crow past still exert on the present can only be remedied by the present generation, or by future generations. The generations which presided over them can do nothing. It is up to us. And it is our responsibility. There are ways we can make it better for all. We should be united in the effort, not divided.

44. The Constant March

"Improved Social Security, affordable, quality healthcare for all, a job for anyone whose current job has been eliminated for whatever reason, a livable wage in any job which would include the ability to save and plan for the future, great public education all the way through college or vocational training, continuing education for all, and most importantly, full participation for all. No marginalized communities. These would all be products of this Progressive philosophy."

It never has been a feature of the New Deal, or Progressivism, or even Socialism or LBJ's Great Society, to continuously give free handouts to poor people. It has never been a feature of any of these to encourage laziness. These have always been false accusations, sometimes heartless and vicious, but mostly just the result of misinformation. The goal is and always has been exactly the opposite—to inspire people to develop their own talents and work both individually and collectively to create a great home for us all.

It is actually the current, ultra-pure, trickle-down capitalistic model that gives unearned, free handouts to people. As we've seen, these handouts go to extremely wealthy people, in a continuous flow, well after they have "earned" any due wealth.

Making the system work for working people is essentially a case of making corrections on the extreme misdistribution of wealth. The New Deal, Progressive model would work through reinforcing already existing programs and creating new ones that provide jobs and social securities.

The government, and extended public sector, must be a major player as an employer. We, together, as the public sector, must also be buyers and sellers just as private individuals are. This results in an additional layer of transactions, millions of them, where money changes hands often, and thus income occurs for millions of people. But it has the added benefit of not requiring excessive and wasteful consumerism to keep the money circulating. People can spend and save and invest while the currency continues to circulate. There are things that we as a society, want and need, just as there are things that individuals want and need. The things that society wants and needs are often not the things that private investors will invest in, because they are not profit-oriented items. They don't produce profit for an investor, but they do produce good for society. A vibrant public sector is the way to ensure that meaningful employment exists throughout the society.

Among the many benefits of this strategy would be the ability to direct people into needed occupations that are not necessarily profitable to the private sector, but extremely needed by society. This could include things like incentives and financial assistance for all levels of medical school and training. Through our current ultra-profit driven healthcare system, way too much money goes to the insurance industry and its stockholders and CEOs and way too little goes into reducing the shortages of actual medical personnel. But let me add that we should make any transition to a better "healthcare for all" system go smoothly for all of those who are currently employed in the private insurance industry.

An additional benefit is that, through government employment, we could ensure that high unemployment will *never* occur. It would also make it much easier to make sure working people earn livable wages. Once again, the private sector will be alive and well, and will benefit from this constant economic stimulus. The only difference is that those who benefit *most* from this economy, i.e., those who are extremely well overcompensated, would pay back some of this over-compensation through a fairer tax system. They would still be wealthy capitalists.

Improved Social Security, affordable, quality healthcare for all, a job for anyone whose current job has been eliminated for whatever reason, a livable wage in any job which would include the ability to save and plan for the future, great public education all the way through college or vocational training, continuing education for all, and most importantly, full participation for all, all of these can be achieved while simultaneously keeping the economy going and promoting entrepreneurialism and free enterprise. There would be no marginalized communities in this scheme. These would all be products of this Progressive philosophy. And with it all comes a thriving community of customers for entrepreneurs with great ideas—entrepreneurs who will contribute back a portion of their reward to this very system that rewards them so greatly. They will continue to be rewarded well.

We, the people, can provide for each other a great system of social securities and at the same time, a wonderful environment for business and enterprise, all through the same simple, unified concept: An Economy for All.

Progressivism, as we define it, is a program with purpose. The purpose being to end all oppression, and build a United Country and an Economy for All.

P. S. *It's past time to do it again, and this time, make it a permanent. There should never be less than 80% of the people voting for an economy for all. There should never be more than 20% voting for oligarchy. A vote for ultra-pure, unbridled capitalism is a vote for oligarchy, i.e., feudalism. Of course, I even think the oligarchs and the would-be oligarchs should vote for an economy for all. They would live in a better world, too. They could still be richer than most of us. This has nothing to do with jealousy. It has everything to do with making life better for everyone.*

The House Is Still Standing

The house is still standing, but we've much to do
It's once more divided, we must think anew
Let us remember, and note, what he said
Take increased devotion from these honored dead
Oh, oh,
Can we be sure
That this nation can long endure
Oh, oh,
Can we nobly save
The last best hope on earth
Abraham Lincoln was cheerful that day
The old melancholy was melting away
The war, it was over, so now celebrate
With malice toward none he walked into his fate
And then
Oh, Oh,
The whole world did cry
As, oh,

That one more soldier did die
In a war that seems to go on
A nation that's governed
By the people
For the people
One nation for all of us
Oh, oh
Will it ever be so?
We need to know
Can we make this work for us all

Available on Spotify and Apple music, Gary Frank Taylor

Appendix

House majority, Senate majority, and Highest tax brackets over the years (one year periods):

Year	House	Senate	President	Tax
1921	R	R	R	58%
1922	R	R	R	58%
1923	R	R	R	58%
1924	R	R	R	46%
1925	R	R	R	25%
1926	R	R	R	25%
1927	R	R	R	25%
1928	R	R	R	25%
1929	R	R	R	25%
1930	R	R	R	25%
1931	R	R	R	25%
1932	R	R	R	63%

From 1921 to 1933, Republicans had majorities in both the House and the Senate. They also held the presidency throughout the period and had the majority in the Supreme Court. Laissez-faire economics (aka trickle-down) was their philosophy. Note the higher tax rates at the beginning of the 12-year period, probably to pay-off WWI debt. But by 1925 the highest bracket had been lowered to 25%. At the end of 1929, the relatively unregulated market crashed, and the Great Depression began. The Republicans continued to believe the economy would come back without government interference, but the Depression got worse. Most historians agree 1929-1933 were the worst years of the Depression.

1933	D	D	D	63%
1934	D	D	D	63%
1935	D	D	D	63%
1936	D	D	D	79%
1937	D	D	D	79%
1938	D	D	D	79%
1939	D	D	D	79%
1940	D	D	D	79%
1941	D	D	D	81%
1942	D	D	D	88%
1943	D	D	D	88%
1944	D	D	D	94%
1945	D	D	D	94%
1946	D	D	D	91%
1947	R	R	D	91%
1948	R	R	D	91%
1949	D	D	D	91%
1950	D	D	D	91%
1951	D	D	D	91%
1952	D	D	D	92%
1953	R	R	R	92%
1954	R	R	R	91%
1955	D	D	R	91%
1956	D	D	R	91%

In 1933, Franklin Roosevelt, promising a pro-active, Progressive government that would work to end the suffering of the Depression, wins the presidency and the Democratic Party wins majorities in both the House and the Senate. Democrats held on to these majorities in both the House and the Senate for all but 4 of the next 48 years.

The newly-elected Democratic President and Congress made immediate and sweeping changes, beginning in 1933, and put the government to work for the people – that is, they used government to help people out in their time of need. When told that the market, without government influence, would bring the economy back in the long run, FDR's trusted advisor, Harry Hopkins, famously said, "People don't eat in the long run; they eat every day". The Republican approach of laissez-faire economics can sound good on the surface, but it is not called trickle-down for nothing. As Hopkins implied, people in need, need to be relieved of stress and poverty ASAP, not in some far-off, promised, abstract future that never arrives for many.

In his April 14, 1938, Fireside Chat, FDR said:
"If you think back to the experiences of the early years of this Administration you will remember the doubts and fears expressed about the rising expenses of Government. But to

1957	D	D	R	91%
1958	D	D	R	91%
1959	D	D	R	91%
1960	D	D	R	91%
1961	D	D	D	91%
1962	D	D	D	91%
1963	D	D	D	91%
1964	D	D	D	77%
1965	D	D	D	70%
1966	D	D	D	70%
1967	D	D	D	70%
1968	D	D	D	70%
1969	D	D	R	70%
1970	D	D	R	70%
1971	D	D	R	70%
1972	D	D	R	70%
1973	D	D	R	70%
1974	D	D	R	70%
1975	D	D	R	70%
1976	D	D	R	70%
1977	D	D	D	70%
1978	D	D	D	70%
1979	D	D	D	70%
1980	D	D	D	70%

the surprise of the doubters, as we proceeded to carry on the program which included Public Works and Work Relief, the country grew richer instead of poorer."

During these years, 1933-1981, when the Democrats controlled Congress, much was accomplished. In addition to the New Deal programs at the beginning of those years – programs that immediately put millions to work during the Depression – they created Social Security and the FDIC, instituted the methods to pay for and win WWII, instituted the methods to win the peace by helping to rebuild Europe with the Marshall plan, gave us the GI Bill (an incredible concept that prevented a slide back into depression), gave us Medicare and Medicaid, supported and built a world class public education system, made major strides in ending Jim Crow laws (with more still to be done), and strides in ending other racial discrimination (with more still to be done), and the list goes on and on.

The government of 1933-1981 did improve people's lives. It was a government that helped people help themselves while simultaneously stimulating the economy. It was a government that paid for these things with an appropriate tax structure. It was a governmental and economic model that worked. The only thing that ever slowed it down at times was those who resisted the model.

1981	D	R	R	70%	The election of Ronald Reagan ushered in a return to Laissez-faire, trickle-down economics philosophies. It was the end of the long line of Democratic majorities in the House and Senate. The 1986 Tax Reform act lowered the top income tax bracket to 28% by 1988. The philosophy returned to the idea of mostly letting the market run itself. Because of Ronald Reagan's influence, Democrats had to either become more conservative, or at least had to appear more conservative during most of this period (1981-2021), particularly on economics. "Liberal" became a bad word during this time. Beginning in 1995, Republicans had another extended run as the majority party in both the House and the Senate. Democrat Bill Clinton was the President at the beginning of this Republican era, and perhaps held things partially in check. When Republican George W. Bush was elected President, the return to laissez-faire, trickle-down economic policy with deregulation in the market was essentially completed. In 2007, the period known as the Great Recession appears. As in the 1929 crash and subsequent Great Depression, this too occurred during an era of Republican dominance. Luckily, Social Security and the FDIC, products of the New Deal, Progressive economic era kept many from losing everything, and was at least partly the reason the recession did not become a full-scale depression. The Progressives of the 1930s had built a safety net that saved many people over 70 years later.
1982	D	R	R	50%	
1983	D	R	R	50%	
1984	D	R	R	50%	
1985	D	R	R	50%	
1986	D	R	R	50%	
1987	D	D	R	38.5%	
1988	D	D	R	28%	
1989	D	D	R	28%	
1990	D	D	R	28%	
1991	D	D	R	31%	
1992	D	D	R	31%	
1993	D	D	D	39.6%	
1994	D	D	D	39.6%	
1995	R	R	D	39.6%	
1996	R	R	D	39.6%	
1997	R	R	D	39.6%	
1998	R	R	D	39.6%	
1999	R	R	D	39.6%	
2000	R	R	D	39.6%	
2001	R	Tie	R	39.1%	
2002	R	Tie	R	38.6%	
2003	R	R	R	35%	
2004	R	R	R	35%	
2005	R	R	R	35%	
2006	R	R	R	35%	
2007	D	Tie	R	35%	
2008	D	Tie	R	35%	
2009	D	D	D	35%	
2010	D	D	D	35%	
2011	R	D	D	35%	
2012	R	D	D	35%	
2013	R	D	D	39.6%	
2014	R	D	D	39.6%	
2015	R	R	D	39.6%	
2016	R	R	D	39.6%	
2017	R	R	R	39.6%	
2018	R	R	R	37%	
2019	D	R	R	37%	
2020	D	R	R	37%	
2021	D	Tie	D	37%	
2022	D	Tie	D	37%	
2023	R	Tie	D	37%	

The chart above is a compilation of data that I believe can be useful to all voters, but particularly to Democratic candidates. The columns under the headings "House" and "Senate" denote the party that held a majority in each of those chambers during the time period given in the first column. The chart was created to demonstrate, what I believe, are several important facts. The most important being that Democrats can begin to make good on their own promises and make life better for all Americans only when they have majorities in the House and Senate, as well as a Democratic president. The candidates need to help people understand what the Democrats can accomplish with these majorities. Interpreting the data requires some additional information. And, of course, out of necessity, we must realize that reality is always more complex than our explanations of it in our attempts to explain it. But it's the best we can do.

I think it is fair to say that, at least since 1921, the economic philosophies of the two major parties are relatively well-defined for those who study it objectively. The simplest way to state it is that Republicans favor laissez-faire economics and Democrats favor what is often described as progressive economics. That is to say that Republicans favor little to no government interference in the economy and low taxes, particularly for the wealthy, while Democrats favor government involvement in the economy and a tax structure that will support it. Republicans claim that the market is self-regulating and that lower taxes for the wealthy will create more jobs. Democrats believe that the laissez-faire approach is inherently unfair, favoring big business, large corporations, and the wealthy.

The laissez-faire approach is often characterized, usually by its critics, as "trickle-down", while the progressive approach is characterized, usually by its critics, as "tax and spend".

Turning our attention to the chart, we easily determine three basic political eras: An era of Republican dominance (1921-1933), an era of Democratic dominance (1933-1981), and an era of back-and-forth, mostly divided government (1981-2024). The Republican Party had control of both houses and the presidency, and even the Supreme Court, from 1921 to 1933. The Democratic Party dominated the legislative branch from 1933 to 1981 and held the presidency most of that period. The third period, 1981-2024, we see that no party has been as dominant as in these previous two periods. But Republicans have held longer extended majorities in the legislative branch.

When it comes to economic philosophy, however, there are only two basic trends. The laissez-faire economic policy was dominant during the 1921-1933 era. The progressive economic policy was dominant during the 1933 – 1981 era. But during the divided government era of 1981-2024, we have returned mostly to the laissez-faire approach. So, my interpretation is that the Republican Party has maintained the most economic influence during this period of divided government. This in turn means that the super wealthy and large corporations have had the most economic influence. Their trickle-down philosophy, which is better termed a gushing up philosophy, as in the money gushes upward, has been the dominating feature of the period, with a few life-saving securities leftover from the Progressive era of 1933-1981.

My belief is that under a laissez-faire economy, wealth begets more wealth. I think we all are aware of the widening economic gap that has been growing ever since the return to laissez-faire economic policy. I usually refer to it as unbridled capitalism. And I think this next point is extremely important:

Under a system where a very few people become extremely wealthy in comparison to most of the population, those few extremely wealthy persons become, in a sense, an unelected "branch" of the government itself. They have a vastly disproportionate influence over the economy as a whole, and of the well-being, or lack thereof, of the vast majority of the people.

I believe that no democratic nation would vote for such a policy if the majority of the voters were aware that that is what was happening. Non-wealthy voters who unknowingly support it are actually voting for their own votes to have diminished value. They are also voting against their own best interests and those of their fellow citizens. With follow-up data in a future post, I will endeavor to demonstrate that at least 70% of the people would benefit from the more progressive approach. And therefore, I believe at least 70% of the people should vote for it. But let me add, that I think it would actually result in a better life for all, and therefore, I believe that 100% of the people should vote for it.

When we observe, from the chart, the information given for the years 1933-1981, we see that there were high tax brackets for the highest incomes for the entire period. When we study American history during that period, we see that that was the period in which the U.S. secured its position as the undisputed number one economy in the world. At the beginning of the period, the new philosophy was immediately put in place by the Roosevelt administration and the new Democratic Congress as the way to combat the Great Depression. While some would argue that placing higher taxes on the wealthy hurts the economy and discourages investment, this entire 48-year period proves that it does not. It literally proves that it does not. In mathematics, to prove a general statement can be very difficult and requires great care and can never be considered "absolute". But to disprove a general statement, it only takes one specific example to show that it is not true. As stated above, the entire period from 1933 to 1981 is the specific example that proves that higher tax brackets do not ruin the economy.

It is also beneficial to notice the accomplishments of the economic philosophy practiced during the 1933 to 1981 period. It began with government work programs like the CCC and the WPA, as well as an insurance program, the FDIC, to ensure that people would not lose their savings in a bank failure, which also had the effect of keeping many banks from failing. By 1935, Social Security was created. The worst years of the Depression were 1929-1933, during which the laissez-faire policies were still dominant. Beginning with the election of Roosevelt and a Democratic Congress, the worst was over. It was still an up and down struggle throughout the 1930s due to many reasons, including a temporary backing off of New Deal (Progressive) philosophy in 1937-38. But as WWII approached, government spending increased even more, and when the government spends money domestically, it is income for the citizens. So, this spending did not cause a backslide into further depression, it apparently did just the opposite. It ended it once and for all.

After the war, there was concern that the Depression would reappear. But wonderful New Deal – style policies that required enormous government spending worked to prevent another backslide. The GI Bill was probably the primary economic driver of this boon to the economy. The Progressive era, 1933-1981, also saw the growth of a world – class public education system, the creations of Medicare and Medicaid, the Civil rights acts of the '60s which began to dismantle the Jim Crow era laws and put an end to various types of discrimination. All of this was done while maintaining a nation of innovative entrepreneurship.

As noted in the table above, from 1933-1981, progressive ideas were being advanced. However, it is important to understand that black Americans were often left out in the early days of this Progressive era, particularly in some states, but also generally throughout the nation. But it was during this 48 year Progressive era that the Civil rights movement gained strength and finally resulted in the 1960s civil rights acts. However, when the civil rights bills became law during LBJ's administration, the parties began to polarize over these ideas, and 1920s-style unbridled capitalism became the hallmark of the Republican Party again. It was the beginning of the stalling, and sometimes backwards motion in progressivism and Civil Rights.

Was the unbridled capitalism of the previous era, 1921-1933, the cause of the Great Depression? I believe so, and I think many, if not most, economists believe it was either the cause, or highly contributed to it.

My belief is that we need an economy that doesn't just promise the potential for a safe and secure economic *future* for each individual or family, but rather one that provides a safe and secure situation for each individual or family at *every* point in their lives. I believe at least 70% of the people would be much better off with a return to the Democratic, Progressive – style approach, truly a government for the people. If we, the people, can vote-in large Democratic majorities in both the House and Senate, as well as elect a Democratic President, then we can work to build a government of the people, by the people, and for the people. That is, if the Democrats will fully return to the Progressive era, New Deal model.

About the Author

When Gary was 19 years old, he married Donna, his high school sweetheart. They had 46 wonderful years of marriage. Together they raised 3 daughters, all beautiful inside and out. They have 3 beautiful grandchildren and one gorgeous great-granddaughter. Donna passed away in September of 2019. Gary says losing her was the most difficult thing he ever experienced in life.

Gary has a master's degree in mathematics, and has studied history just as extensively. He spent a total of 25 years as a public high school and community college math teacher, and 3 years in private schools, including a year at the university level. As of this writing, he is a candidate for Congress. By the time you read this, the primary will be over, and he will either be relaxing, or preparing for the general election.

Gary says, "I care deeply about making this country work for everybody, and I care deeply about my generation leaving the world better than we found it. We need to hurry. I am not entering politics as a career. I have had my career. I enter because I want to do what I can to make a difference. I want my children and grandchildren, and all of us, to look forward to a great future in the good old USA – in a much more united, United States."

Gary is also a musician. His music website is garyfranktaylor.com

Campaign website: garytaylorforcongress.com

His music is available on both Apple and Spotify under Gary Frank Taylor.

The above is written in third person, but Gary wrote it himself.

Made in the USA
Coppell, TX
21 March 2026

74401478R00089